Best to you
in all your endeavors!

Tom Elliott

Business Survival in an Internet Economy

Website 411

A Plain Language Explanation of What You
Should Know about Doing Business Online

Thomas M. Elliott

Website 411: Business Survival in an Internet Economy
Copyright © 2008 by Thomas M. Elliott

Library of Congress Control Number: 2007942012
ISBN 0-7414-4455-0

This edition published by:

INFINITY
PUBLISHING.COM

by arrangement with Thomas M. Elliott

1094 New DeHaven Street, Suite 100
West Conshohocken, PA 19428-2713
Info@buybooksontheweb.com
www.buybooksontheweb.com
Toll-free (877) BUY BOOK
Local Phone (610) 941-9999
Fax (610) 941-9959

First Printing: 2008
Printed and bound in the United
States of America
Printed on Recycled Paper
Published January 2008

Trademarks

The following trademarks appear throughout this book: Adobe Dreamweaver, Adobe Flash, Adobe GoLive, Google, Microsoft FrontPage, Microsoft MSN, The Website Triangle, Sun Microsystems JavaScript, Yahoo!

All terms mentioned in this book that are known to be trademarks or service marks have been appropriately capitalized and belong to their respective companies. Infinity Publishing cannot attest to the accuracy of this information. Use of a term in this book should not be regarded as affecting the validity of any trademark or service mark.

Disclaimer

Every effort has been made to make this book as complete and correct as possible, but no warranty of fitness is implied. The information is provided on an as-is basis. The author and Infinity Publishing assume no liability nor any responsibility with respect to any loss or damages arising from the information contained in this book. Readers should consult a qualified Website consultant for specific applications and updated information to meet their particular requirements.

Colleges, corporations, and non-profit organizations

Quantity discounts are available on bulk purchase of this book for educational training purposes, fund-raising, or gift giving. For information contact WebDrafter.com, Inc. P.O. Box 112, Millerstown, PA 17062, (866)421-3723 or visit *www.Website411Book.com*.

To Brittni A. Linn
        My Princess
To Melodi
        My loving, patient and supportive wife

Contents

iv

Paradigm

par•a•digm [**par**-uh-dahym, -dim]

(noun)
1. An example serving as a model; pattern
2. A set of assumptions, concepts, values, and practices that constitute a way of viewing reality for the community that shares them.

Paradigm Shift

(noun)
1. A fundamental change in approach or assumptions which alters widely accepted patterns and practices.

Foreword

I have often been told that I should write a book. But in my mind there were very few topics on computers and the Internet that remained unexplored or unexploited. Once a bookstore is populated with one or two classic "how to" references on a particular topic, the shelves seem to be quickly overloaded with a flood of "me too" texts, almost overnight. I didn't want to contribute to the demise of any more forests by printing a ditto version of someone else's work.

Recently, however, a new pattern has emerged in the business world that is relatively undocumented in the marketplace. It's a disturbing trend, and it relates directly to the Internet, Websites, and e-commerce. Many businesses are forging ahead using technology to either start a pure Internet venture or to embrace their existing brick-and-mortar establishments. At the same time, traditional businesses *without* an Internet presence are closing their doors at an alarmingly *increasing* rate. Surprisingly, relatively few business owners are taking the time to effectively identify why their businesses are falling down the economic ladder or failing altogether.

Many businesses are struggling or going out of business because they find it impossible or too difficult to keep up with the competition. Further examination reveals that in many (most) instances, their *competition* has a Web presence. Is it merely coincidence? Arguably, there is a direct correlation in today's business world. Smaller profit margins and higher overhead are forcing the hand of traditional businesses (storefront and otherwise) in the matter, and they are increasingly yielding to *businesses with Websites* that work smarter, not harder. Not only is their demise unfortunate, it is completely unnecessary.

My purpose in writing this book is twofold: to bridge the gap between fear and technology; and to educate business decision makers about the recent economic paradigm shift commonly known as the *Internet Revolution* which is silently but profoundly affecting their bottom line. The bottom line it's affecting could be *yours*.

In most cases, I have found that people avoid doing things that they don't understand, and they avoid investing time or money in anything if they feel someone might take advantage of them. I enjoy helping business people by demystifying Websites and the Internet marketplace (e-commerce) so they understand how simple it all really can be.

Whether you are new in business or have been around for years, understanding the Internet's impact on your company is critical to your future and continued success.

If you don't already have a site, it may be because costs are a prevailing concern or you do not see the immediate need for one. In prioritizing your time, perhaps setting up a Website falls low on the list. Or you may simply be procrastinating on getting a Website because you are uncomfortable with, confused by, or intimidated by the technical nature of the Internet.

If you already have a Website for your business or organization, you will benefit from this book by learning how to make your site more effective. Perhaps you are having trouble with your current Web developer, or you may simply be unsure of what a Website can offer you.

Maybe yours is one of the thousands of businesses misrepresented by a less-than-effective Website; the difference between online success and failure can often be a simple matter of adjusting your existing Web presence.

Despite the title, this is not a technical book. It is a book about why it makes sense to integrate a Web presence into your business and how to go about doing so effectively. Although it covers some topics that relate to technology, this book is a plain English approach to doing business in a Website era.

It is designed to be a "quick read." I suggest that you read it straight through the first time and then refer back to the section tabs on the edge of each page to find key information in the future. The tabs are arranged to cover the following categories:

- **Website Basics:** concepts and fundamentals you should know about Websites as they relate to your business
- **Your Options:** factors and considerations to explore with regard to establishing a Web presence that meets your needs
- **Questions & Answers:** what to ask solution providers and what they should tell you about features, benefits, and services to enhance your business on the Internet
- **The Decision Process:** how to deliberately and methodically establish your business on the Internet

- **Marketing:** traditional and online methods to promote your business, ensuring you earn a return on your Web investment
- **Your Next Step:** resources and follow-up steps to maximize your Website's potential while keeping up with emerging business trends

Because this book may be used as a quick reference, there is some intentional redundancy between sections. Many elements of a complete Web solution interrelate, so where appropriate, relevant content is repeated in summary from section to section within the context of each topic.

I'm aware that you are busy, your time is valuable, and you simply "need to know what you need to know." When you are done reading this book, you will have a solid business understanding of:

- what to expect from a Web presence
- how to ensure your Website meets your needs
- how to evaluate Website proposals
- how to avoid being oversold or undersold in the process of establishing a Website
- how to cost effectively advertise using the Internet

Whether you decide to move forward with doing business online or not, you will have a solid understanding of today's online marketplace and how the Internet is affecting traditional businesses.

Text boxes are used throughout this book to help you learn. Here are the symbols used and what they mean:

The mouse symbol is used to summarize points made within a section.

The skull and crossbones caution you about actions or behaviors that may be counterproductive to your success online.

The smiley face is used to make favorable recommendations which should enhance your online success.

Thumbs-up indicates an advantage or benefit.

Thumbs-down indicates a disadvantage or drawback.

Section One: The Basics

Topics covered:

The Need to Venture Online

What a Website Can Do for You

The Importance of Finding
Your Website

Ensuring Your Site
Is User-Friendly

and

The Website Triangle™

A Sign of the Times

Did they have a Website? No.
Cause and effect? There is likely a correlation.

Doing Business on the Web: A Necessity?

Do You Really Need to Venture Online?

Why should you consider doing business on the Internet? More specifically, do you need a Website? These are important questions. If you are starting up a new company or store, the answer to each seems pretty simple: everyone else is getting Websites and you need one to be competitive. But if you have been established for awhile, the answer may not be as obvious without looking at emerging consumer trends in the marketplace. If you own a small to medium-size business and currently have more customers than you can handle, or if you have a highly seasonal business, you may feel that you do *not* need to establish a presence online (but keep reading to be sure).

You must decide conclusively whether *your* business needs a Website now when it never needed one before. You will probably decide that it *does* need one eventually, but either way you choose, you should be comfortable that you are making an informed decision and the *right* decision for your business.

The next time you attend a networking social, mixer, or Chamber of Commerce event, take note of the others who are there. Notice that the average, *established* business owner is someone between the ages of 35 and 60 who started their venture several years ago. Perhaps he or she started a job shortly after high school or college, then started a company after gaining experience working for someone else. Or perhaps that person took over the family business. There are dozens of scenarios, but regardless of how they got started, one detail is true for each of them: years ago, they didn't need a Website to survive. In fact, depending on how long ago their business began, Websites and the Internet may not have even existed.

Websites are popular, but just because a new advertising tool exists, you should not blindly run out and buy it. If you were successful in business for years without a Website, you're probably wondering why you might suddenly need one now. You may even be steadfastly opposed to having one, especially if computers, technology and the Internet make you uncomfortable. Some business owners even see Websites merely as sales gimmicks or a passing fad.

I would not expect you to spend any money on something that would provide no value or to buy a Website without understanding how it would benefit your business. Instead, let me offer you this suggestion: do not make your decision to buy or not to buy an online solution based on the newness or your comfort level with Websites. Make your decision based on *the shopping habits and lifestyle habits of your most important asset: your customers.*

Times have changed. Years ago in the average family, one parent worked a job during the day while the other managed the household. That's the kind of family that I grew up in myself. While the kids were in school, the at-home parent took care of running household errands, paying bills, and shopping for the family's needs.

There weren't any Websites, so people found what they needed through the phone book or from driving around store to store. In the evening, people relaxed and enjoyed family time after supper. After-hours shopping was more of a leisurely activity or social event. Life was a bit simpler then, wouldn't you agree?

Nowadays, not only have lifestyles changed, but spending and shopping habits have changed as well. Household economics are different than they were when television shows like *Leave It to Beaver* or *The Brady Bunch* depicted the ideal way of life. As a nation, large families have given way to single parents, couples without kids, and smaller families with two or fewer children.

Dual income families are prevalent now with both parents working or single parents holding down two or more jobs to make ends meet. People are busier than they used to be, with more crowded schedules and less time for family. Consequently there are fewer shoppers running household errands during the day because more people are working longer hours to help them subsist through the more expensive cost of living.

By the time parents are home from work, dinner is over, the homework is done, scarce family time comes to an end, and the kids are tucked in bed, what time do you suppose it is?

In the average family, it's between eight and nine o'clock at night. And what time does the average brick-and-mortar business close? Perhaps a better question is this: what time does *your* business close at night?

Most businesses today still close sometime between 5 pm and 9 pm, right about when the average consumer is finally available to take some personal time to decompress after their busy day. Perhaps that explains why prime time shopping hours on the Internet are from 9 pm to 11 pm each night, when people are finally able to relax, shop, find what they want, and either buy it online or locate the store where they will go to make their purchase in a spare moment. Your customers are *moonlighting*, literally, when they shop.

Time has become everyone's scarcest resource. It is increasingly more difficult for people to budget time to shop during normal business hours when stores are open, especially when consumers are challenged with trying to balance work life with home life. The most important point to remember in order to keep your market share is that you must *sell* the way your customers *shop*, or they will *buy* from *someone else*.

It's important that you fully grasp the significance of the fact that people do more than their shopping online; they do their *research* online. They figure out where they'll go to buy what they need, whether it is a product or service, by first searching for a business that has a Website. If your business is closed by 9 pm and you don't have a Website, you're not even on the list of places being considered. As far as the customer is concerned, you're transparent—not even in business. In their virtual shopping experience, your long-time established business simply *doesn't exist.*

The alarming part about it is that if you do nothing to remedy the situation, your virtual (online) non-existence could well become a self-fulfilling prophesy in the physical, brick-and-mortar sense. Before long, you could be out of business if you can't attract new and existing customers who regularly use and depend upon the Internet. Your years of hard work developing a strong reputation simply don't matter to the *online* customer if you do not have a Website.

You might shop online yourself occasionally, but you may not be making the connection between your business's daily operations and Internet economic trends. After all, if you have spent the last several years open for business within the same four walls, day-in and day-out, never needing a Website to remain profitable, you may not be in tune with the cultural changes in your customers' evolving shopping and spending habits due to the Internet. How would you even know that your business is potentially threatened by this significant paradigm shift? Well, you *wouldn't* know.

Why not? Because the *cause* happened almost overnight, but the *effects* took place very gradually. Prior to the mid-1990's, Internet traffic was mostly limited to government and educational institutions. The commercialization of the Internet and the dot-com boom brought about changes that made many business owners realize that a Website adds a new dimension to customer service as well as retailing.

Now that doing business on the Web is commonplace, businesses without Websites frequently feel a financial pinch that is reflected in their profit and loss reports.

For the business owner who continues to be financially constricted over time, the tendency may be to throw money at traditional forms of advertising that worked well in the past, such as phone book ads, billboards, flyers and Sunday newspaper coupons. In today's marketplace, these advertisements are losing steam

7

due to their higher costs and progressively lower returns on investment compared to Internet methods.

The effects of the growing Internet economy are quietly creeping up on unsuspecting businesses so gradually that many business owners fail to make the correlation between declining profits and the escalation of doing business online. When there is a paradigm shift in the marketplace, businesses that adapt quickly survive, whereas others that cling to what has always been familiar slowly decline to the point of failure.

We can see several examples of how slow-to-respond business giants became dwarfed by up-and-coming industries that created paradigm shifts. The typewriter industry all but collapsed with the advent of word processing and computers. Swiss watch companies that were world-famous for precision timepieces were decimated by the invention of digital watches. Small corner stores like butchers, drug stores, and malt shops were crowded out by mega-stores that offered one-stop shopping.

In each case, something happened in the market that prompted the affected industry to experience a fundamental change in how they did business. Companies that failed to adapt accordingly became casualties to their competition.

Often times, marketplace changes are caused by two or more seemingly unrelated factors that pressure an industry. For example, hybrid gas-electric vehicles are emerging in the auto industry to replace gas-only vehicles as car manufacturers respond to recent consumer demands due to 1) inflated gas prices and 2) increased environmental awareness.

To give another example, businesses are migrating to the Internet today due to widespread *consumer Internet access* and *computers being commonplace in most households*. As a result, businesses that are not online are losing money to businesses that have Websites.

A "stop the bleeding" approach to recover from an economic downturn (or even a plateau) can be dangerous if you don't know essential information about today's marketing opportunities and Web economics, coined *Webinomics*. The Internet economy is booming, expanding by leaps and bounds at a rate of 20% to 25% growth each year. Consider that the escalating trend of moonlighting customers likely translates to an increasing number of empty parking spaces in your parking lot.

The bottom line is this: *for your business to stay successful, you must adjust your selling habits to match the changes in consumer buying habits.* That means that your business probably needs a Website.

To further illustrate the point, I'll share the story of a residential painter in Sterling, Virginia, whose van was parked curbside in front of a neighbor's house. His business name, address and phone number were on the side of his vehicle, but there was no Website address displayed. I had some window trim that needed to be painted, so I asked the painter for his business card—again, no Website address.

As typical consumers do today, I asked him for his Web address (making the assumption that he had one) so I could see samples of his work, any customer testimonials, and more information on the services he provided. What I received, instead, sounded like a well-rehearsed, rapid-fire speech delivered in almost a single breath that went something like this:

I don't have a Website. I don't need one. I've never had to have one because most of my customers are word-of-mouth. I have plenty of business. Plus, I don't care if someone finds me on the Internet outside of this area—I'm not going to go to California to paint someone's house. I'm just a one-man-show, and a Website would be a waste of money to me.

He had undoubtedly been asked dozens (or hundreds) of times about having a Website before I innocently asked the question. Rather than argue with him, I invited him inside to discuss the work that needed to be done (and to show him something about Websites that hadn't occurred to him).

We went on the Internet, and I did a quick search using the keywords "Residential Painters in Sterling VA". Within seconds, the computer screen was filled with painters in the local area. He immediately recognized his competition and was bewildered at the simplicity and speed with which everybody's businesses *but* his were displayed for me to consider.

A moment before, I had been his potential customer. Suddenly he experienced a sense of loss as he realized how many local jobs he must be missing on a monthly basis. I clicked on a few of the sites that were listed, and after browsing portfolios of their jobs, I asked him which of them he would have recommended to me if I hadn't walked next door to speak with him.

10

He got the point. His next words, sheepishly, were "I don't need an *expensive* Website, do I?"

The biggest deterrent associated with owning a Website is the assumption that it must be expensive to get started. It's a myth. A Website can be very affordable.

If your business is doing well right now, consider how doing business online would further enhance your financial position. A Website works as an interactive, automated marketing tool, and it can serve as *multiple* storefronts by connecting with links from other Websites around the Internet. In other words, you bear the cost of establishing your business on the Web initially, and gradually dozens or perhaps hundreds of other sources link to you at no additional expense.

The more businesses that point to your Website, the more free advertising you receive. In the long-run, the net operating costs of your Website become insignificant compared to the return on investment that the advertisement delivers. No other form of marketing compounds value and spreads like an effective Website.

On the other hand, if times are financially tight right now and your success is in the balance, you must evaluate how to best confront your fiscal challenges. In such a situation, beware of the "tailspin" thought process that can lead your business to disaster:
1) "I've never needed a Website before."
2) "Websites are probably expensive."
3) "I'm having financial challenges right now."
4) "I need to save money, not spend it."
5) "I won't buy the Website now. Maybe later, when I'm making more money."

If business continues to slump, the aversion to expenses becomes stronger, and the spiral continues. You must do something to break the chain.

Is it possible that the right solution in order to survive in today's economy is to *expand* your business to include the Internet?

Be practical about the whole decision. It's to your advantage to have a small, affordable yet effective Web presence that people can find rather than a fancy one that goes undiscovered. In most cases a simple, brochure-style presence that is marketed well can cost just a few hundred dollars and be a revenue producing, time saving asset for your company. Even some of the more elaborate Websites that allow customers to make purchases online can cost less annually than a typical phone book ad costs monthly.

How the Internet Leads to Your Success:

You are open for business even after your doors are closed for the evening.

You sell the way your customers shop.

Don't fall prey to the mindset that *"if my business is not on the Internet, than the Internet is not affecting my business."* Quite the opposite is true.

Flowchart

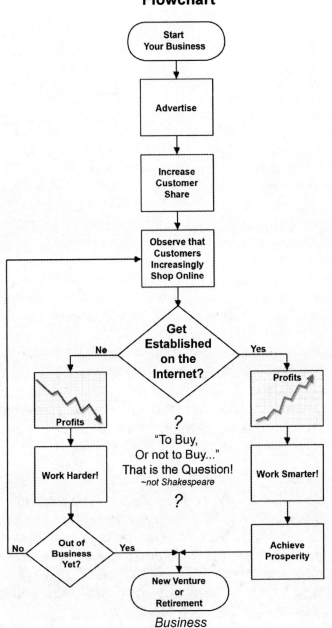

*Business
In Today's Internet Economy*

Website Usefulness: Presence to Profits

What Can Your Website Do for You?

Today, to varying degrees in every industry, the personal touch of a business owner knowing each customer is either gone or is quickly going away. However, the shift away from personal interaction is not one-sided. Your customers are fifteen times more likely to look on the Internet than they are to flip through a phone book to call you. They have become used to turning to the Web. In other words, their shopping and lifestyle habits have changed from when most established businesses started years ago.

Technology has prompted these changes to a large extent. While families have shrunk in size, the cost of living has incrementally increased for each household, resulting in each adult family member bearing a higher share of the expenses for rent, food, utilities, etc. However, an exception to the increasing price trends can be found in the fast-advancing world of electronics. As new gadgetry becomes available, the market is flooded with more affordable equipment that improves consumers' quality of life.

Just a few years ago home technology was limited to a television and a VCR. Today's households are equipped with much of the same tools that were once found only in office environments: computers, fax machines, copiers, and such. Likewise, cellular phones and personal data assistants (PDAs) have become commonplace, replacing old, clunky pagers and providing instant on-the-hip access to voicemail, text messaging, and the Internet. It takes little effort for the average consumer to get on the Web these

14

days, whether they are at work, in the comfort of their own home, or anywhere in between.

Consequently, consumer access to the Internet is *expected* in the marketplace today, and lifestyle changes have driven spending and shopping habits in the direction of e-commerce. The average employee spends their day commuting and working longer hours or trying to manage more than one job to help them afford (or upgrade) their lifestyle in a credit saturated, "buy it now" economy. The result: crowded schedules with competing demands on their calendars and less time for socializing... or for shopping.

But how does the Internet play into all of this? And what is the related impact on *your* business?

Consider the fact that the Internet eliminates limitations of regional time zones and geographical barriers around the world. On a local, national or international scale, a customer can compare pricing and availability of products, services and information from Hong Kong to Dallas to New York City, side-by-side at their kitchen table.

Also consider that there is a three hour time difference across four time zones in the continental United States from Eastern Time to Central Time to Mountain Time to Pacific Time. Shopping from nine o'clock to eleven o'clock at night (prime time shopping hours on the Web) equates to a two hour "rolling" window of time, adding an hour for each time zone crossed from coast to coast. That means that there are effectively five critical shopping hours each weeknight that businesses without Websites cannot account for in today's economy.

Doing the math, in any given five-day work week, the Internet adds 25 *prime time* shopping hours to a business's revenue. For most businesses, that's equivalent to 2+ days of sales per week, or an extra shopping week per month. It's an extra twelve shopping weeks (three months) per year.

If *your* business could do an extra three month's worth of sales each calendar year while your doors were closed and your employees were off the clock, would you be interested? Now consider weekends, *non*-prime time hours, 20 more time zones (including Alaska and Hawaii), and international markets. Remember, the Internet is open 24/7, year-round, globally. *Businesses with Websites have an edge.*

The advantages of doing business on the Internet are not limited to *selling* online. It is a common misconception that Websites are simply high-tech counterparts to in-store cash registers. Service businesses benefit from Websites just as much as retail businesses. True, a Website can serve as a Point of Sale (POS) for your business, but there are so many more uses that the Internet has to offer to help your business become more profitable.

A *well-planned* Internet presence helps your business regardless of whether you sell products or services. Many business owners in service-oriented industries such as hair care, lawn care, law, accounting, insurance, counseling, contracting, real estate, even tattoo parlors—the list doesn't end—sometimes overlook the merit of owning a Website. The common hesitation that impacts decision makers in service companies results from a failure to recognize the connection between the Internet and financial success in their existing brick-and-mortar establishments in today's economy.

Addressing just the few individual types of companies listed on the previous page, the following comments from service-related businesses are typical:

- *"I can't give a haircut online."*
- *"I can't mow and trim a yard online."*
- *"I don't want to give free legal advice online. If I do, the client may never come into my office."*
- *"I need to keep my clients' financial information private and secure, and I can't do their taxes through a Website."*
- *"I don't want to give an insurance quote to a client over the Internet, just to have them compare it with someone else's."*
- *"I can't provide therapy or guidance online. That would be too impersonal, and I need to talk with each client so I can help them with their individual needs."*
- *"I can't hook up plumbing (or electrical) connections online."*
- *"I don't sell houses over the Internet. People want to see the place in person."*
- *"I can't give a tattoo online. Body art is very personal and individualized."*

The list goes on, but the theme remains the same. Even if your particular business model is not mentioned above, you may have had similar reasons *not* to establish a Website. In each of these examples, the unspoken, *mistaken* assumption is that a Website would only provide a benefit to service-oriented businesses if 1) a customer buys directly on the Internet, and 2) the business owner can render their service directly through the Website.

17

Throughout the rest of this section, we'll correct the record as we address these and other concerns.

Changes in consumer shopping habits have made Website usefulness span beyond the sale of products and services. When your potential customer searches for what you have to offer, they want to see something on your Website that establishes credibility and trust.

The more personal the service (hair care, tattoo, financial, counseling, legal, etc.), the more research customers want to do to ensure they are comfortable with the service provider. The more potentially expensive the service (legal, medical, automotive, travel, construction, real estate, etc.), the more comparisons customers want to make to ensure they get the best value for their dollar.

Whether or not prices are cited on your Website, customers look for signs of quality and professionalism. The purpose of your Website is not necessarily to convince your customer to buy on the spot. It may be to encourage them to pick up the phone and ask for more information, speak with an expert, make an appointment, or schedule a free consultation. Realize that *a Website is most often the customer's initial point of contact for your business*.

Clients will turn to your service-related Website to see portfolios of your work, a resumé of your experience, a list of information they need to bring to an appointment, testimonials from existing clients, and more. The clichéd expression, *a picture is worth a thousand words*, applies. People believe what they read and are emotionally impacted by images that they see. When you can present your company in an

18

interesting, colorful, expressive, and interactive way online, you will attract more business.

Of course, one benefit Websites offer is the ability to use the Internet as a source for transactions. Service establishments often offer products, too, as is the case with hair salons. Online billing is also a possibility. With regards to restaurants, dry cleaners, computer repair, and other pay-upon-pick-up businesses, your Website can serve as a pre-payment tool to reduce the time that customers wait in line at the cash register.

Pre-paid orders can be a new, *higher level* of service that you offer, making your business more attractive than your competition's. When customers know that they can walk into your store and simply "grab-and-go," it's much more appealing to them in their busy lifestyles than standing in line elsewhere for three to five minutes behind other customers. A simple 30-second advantage over your competitors can translate to better cash flow and streamlined, more efficient operation of your business.

Your Website works for you even while your attention is focused on the day-to-day management of your business. After-hours, on weekends, and even while you are away on vacation, your Website is dutifully available to potential customers so they can visit your business. It is a marketing tool that people can explore regardless of your business hours.

If you have a seasonal business, consider how you might increase your revenues by using the Internet. Assume your business remains open for five months out of the year, May through September during the summer tourist season along the Ocean City, Maryland, boardwalk. Once the tourist season is over, it would not be cost effective to keep your shop open for regular business hours when you add the costs of electricity, payroll, and other overhead. The majority of your customers would be gone until the next season.

But what if you could sell year-round via online ordering? If a family from Ohio bought from your shop in August, they might conceivably be interested in making another purchase from you in October *if you were open for business and it were convenient for them to do so.* If you had a means of contacting them (using a Website with a customer mailing list tool) to offer them special pricing or a customer loyalty discount for the upcoming holiday season, you would probably get their attention... and earn their purchase.

Along the same line of thought, that family may not take their annual summer vacation to your locale every year. It would be nice if they had a way of buying from you even when their travels were to take them elsewhere. Using an effective Website as a marketing tool, you can convert a one-time, seasonal (or transient) customer into a lifetime business asset, facilitated by the Internet. At the same time, you effectively minimize costs and do not need to maintain the same level of overhead to produce the equivalent net profit in the off-season throughout the year.

Websites convey credibility to consumers similar to how toll-free numbers did years ago. In many ways, your Website will achieve better results for you than a toll-free number would. When people see a phone number, they are not *compelled* to call it. In comparison, Websites intrigue consumers and curiosity leads them to check out Web addresses. There's an interest that prevails when consumers are exposed to a domain name on your current advertising, whether you advertise by broadcast ads or printed material.

Also keep in mind that Websites are dynamic in nature. They're never *done*. Unlike printed catalogs, brochures, and magazine advertisements that cannot be updated once they've hit the printing press, your Internet presence can (and should) be updated regularly. It's a great way to offer specials and promotions to loyal customers and to attract new business with a strong marketing campaign.

One of the most powerful advantages of doing business online is the flexibility to make changes to your site. Updates to your Website can happen in a matter of days, hours, or minutes. The phone book, on the other hand, is only printed once a year so a misprint or outdated information can cost you plenty of business as you wait for the next edition.

Consider the true case of an attorney who had the same first name as another attorney across town, but their last names differed slightly. We'll say one's last name was Friedman, while the other's was Freeman (not their real names). Imagine the dismay when Freeman's phone book ad was mistakenly printed with Friedman's phone number. There is no way to measure how much business Attorney Freeman lost to her competition because of a simple typo that could not be corrected for an entire year.

While we are discussing attorneys, I had an attorney client who was concerned that giving free legal advice on a Website might cause him two major problems. First, he was concerned that he might be liable for malpractice, giving incomplete or inadequate counsel over the Internet without having the specifics on a particular case. Second, he was concerned that he might even lose clients because they might get what they felt they needed from the Website and forego setting up an appointment. After exploring the options, however, the decision became pretty clear that having an Internet presence was the right way to proceed with his law practice.

I asked him a few simple questions about different scenarios that his typical clients would experience: DUIs, criminal arrests, divorces, custody battles, and speeding tickets. My first question was, "What could some of the consequences be for each of the scenarios?" He recited some of the maximum risks and penalties that an individual might experience. My next question to him was, "What should a person do to protect him or herself if they were to be involved in any of those situations?" The answer: *Get a lawyer.*

It was at that moment that he realized that the advice he would post on a Website was simply, "Call Me," not a series of "how-to" legal steps for clients to defend themselves. The marketing strategy was to share the consequences of what *could* happen without representation, and the legal advice was simply to retain legal counsel, followed by the attorney's phone number for a free consultation. By posting the basic, insightful advice to "get a lawyer," his Website serves him well.

The same concept holds true for other professions, including medicine, accounting, engineering, counseling, and any other field where a business owner is paid for expertise or information. The Website is not always the source of the sought-after information. It is the vehicle by which the client finds the expert.

As soon as potential customers find your Website, they begin evaluating whether your business is the right one to meet their needs. Their first impression is important, as is the remainder of their experience visiting your site. Ideally they will bookmark your site by adding it to their list of favorites for future reference, and will continue to visit it for additional purchases and information. If you equip it with tools that make their lives easier or that add value to their Internet browsing experience, that is even better.

An accountant might want to post a "get organized" form on a Website to help clients prepare information for filing taxes. Note that the Website does not provide the actual tax preparation service; it just makes the client's role easier.

An insurance agent may opt to post a quote request form on the site, collecting relevant information on a secure page that protects clients' personal information. Note that the Website does not provide the quote; it provides an interactive tool for the insurance agent to reach the client and request details, saving each of them time.

The same convenience can be offered to professionals in counseling, social services, real estate, and other fields requiring personalized customer service. The Website serves as the tool to connect people together in business.

A common concern among business owners is that Websites are cold and impersonal, eliminating the human element. Doing business on the Internet does not replace customer service; it *supplements* it by helping you manage your customer relationships.

To provide a better idea of how a Website can help you expand your level of customer service, generate revenue, and offer value to your customers, consider the following potential uses. Some of the applicability may only loosely parallel your particular company, but with a little imagination and creative management skills, you will probably find that your business could use a Website to serve your customers in many more ways than just being a high-tech brochure on the Internet. The list is far from all-inclusive. The possibilities are virtually limitless.

Two Dozen and Two Reasons
To Do Business on the Internet

Use or Benefit:	Examples of Applicability:
Answer frequently asked questions	If customers repeatedly ask for information on the same subject matter, your Website can be a central point for answers to their questions. Frequently Asked Questions (FAQs) can pertain to general information such as office hours and location, or they can be specific to your products, services, or specialties.

Use or Benefit:	Examples of Applicability:
Archive your records	The days of microfiche are gone, but paperwork still abounds. Reduce clutter and create an organized, searchable archive of documents for retrieval on demand. A Website based archive is accessible from anywhere in the world. Protect it with a password, or make the files available to the general public. With a secure Website, you can create a library of medical or legal documents, articles, letters, or even entire volumes of books. Make them viewable via a Web page or make them downloadable.
Awareness and exposure	Is there an issue or topic that you need to publicize? Do you have a story to tell masses of people? If you have a public service announcement, the World Wide Web is the most efficient, widespread vehicle to deliver your message. Businesses and organizations use Websites to post policy changes, breaking news, job announcements, upcoming product releases, new services and more.
Become a source of consumer information	Your Website provides a way to send newsletters, helpful tips, and other useful information to your customers. Provide details that customers can sort and display to help them shop. For example, a database of car parts can contain part numbers, measurements, prices, and pictures. A real estate database of houses can be sorted by square footage, price, style, school district, and so forth. Help your customers find what they want.
Build customer loyalty	Keep people aware of (and interested in) your business by using your Website to publicize your establishment and help you manage your customer relations. Offer online discounts to repeat customers to show your appreciation, provide incentives to buy from you, and reward them for their loyalty.

25

Use or Benefit:	Examples of Applicability:
Compound your earnings through affiliates	Word of mouth *used to be* the most powerful form of advertising. No longer. Word of mouth marketing only travels as fast as people talk and is limited to a customer's sphere of influence. Internet marketing travels at the speed of light and has no geographic boundaries. Use your Website to track referral sales of your product or service from other Websites, and reward the source of each transaction with a small percentage of the sale. Money talks; referrals compound.
Create a marketing buzz	Create a sense of urgency by advertising time-sensitive sales, coupons, drawings, contests, or prizes to promote awareness of (and traffic to) your business. As customers visit your site to take advantage of special offers and activities online, expect an increase in referrals to your business.
Credibility through customer testimonials	Do your customers, clients, etc. have positive things to say about you? If you are an author, do people have good reviews of your book? If you are an entertainer, or keynote speaker, do your audiences endorse your stage presence and recommend you to others? Use a dedicated page of testimonials, or intersperse peoples' complimentary comments throughout your site. Even more powerful, link testimonials to audio files that play when clicked upon.

Use or Benefit:	Examples of Applicability:
Display your wares online	Use your Website for swatches or color samples of paint, fabric, stamped concrete patterns, fence styles, vinyl pool liner designs and more. Let your customers use your Website to customize and display various combinations of colors and materials. Whether you work with scrap booking, interior decor, house plans, furniture, or anything that people want to preview as they shop, the sky is the limit on how your customers can experience your available selections through a Website.
Eliminate seasonal or geographic restrictions to your income	Don't rely on local tourism or favorable weather. Use your Website to overcome your typical market limitations. Sell ski gear in August. Although it may be summer in the United States, it's cold below the Equator. Think internationally. What if you had a bakery on the boardwalk along the east coast? Even after the tourists leave and the weather turns cold, send coffee cakes and fudge to anyone in the country. If you are separated from other towns by miles, mountains or water, your Website bridges the gap and makes your business part of other communities.
Expand into international markets	Offer multi-lingual versions of your Website so culturally diverse customers have equal access to your business in foreign markets. Do business around the globe without adding costs to your marketing efforts.
Improve communications	Letters are obsolete in today's world of instant communications and just-in-time logistics. Get everyone on the same page at the same time, or facilitate a central point for your customers and suppliers to exchange information via your Website. Being in the middle gives you control and access to everyone. Your Website puts you there.

27

Use or Benefit:	Examples of Applicability:
Improve customer service	Add value to your level of service by providing customers with helpful resources. Make instructions and guidance readily available online, so that when people call or visit you, they are ready to do business. No matter what type of organization you have, a Website enhances accessibility for customers, clients, patrons, patients, etc. Offer them better service levels and they will think of *your* business before they think of your competition.
Maintain accountability	Use login pages on your Website to track the sales people who make the best use of their Web-based resources, leads, contact management programs, etc. Manage from a distance using Website statistics to identify who your superstars are. Use your Website to focus your management attention where it is needed most and to reward your top performers. Eliminate the guesswork of who is doing the heavy lifting and who isn't pulling their weight in your business.
Manage schedules	If you work with event planning, travel reservations, catering, medical or financial appointments, tournaments, or any other activity coordination, use your Website for customers to request and reserve time slots. Also, use your Website to show patrons, clients, or attendees your upcoming events so they can plan to attend.

28

Use or Benefit:	Examples of Applicability:
Market your collateral services	If you use the phone book to advertise your main products or services under one heading, you can effectively and inexpensively use your Website to increase sales within other categories. Advertise each type of product or service under numerous categories without paying for each individually. Real estate brokers can promote property management and rental services as well as their regular sales listings. Landscapers can advertise irrigation systems, decks and fencing. Car dealerships can promote service and body work. Customers will be able to find your main business when they look for other products and services that you offer.
Measure Return on Investment	Use your Website to monitor responses from your advertisements. Traffic on the Internet is highly measurable allowing you to know how many people visited you online, how they found you, what words they used to look for you, and how long they stayed on your Website. By measuring and monitoring your traffic, you can adjust and control your advertising efforts.
Present material interactively	Your Website can be a teaching tool as well as a learning tool. Post slide shows, pre-recorded seminars, and videos to inform your customers or train your employees. Record weekly sales conference calls for playback on the Web.
Provide informational or technical chat support	Use your Website to provide a discussion forum or interactive chat session. Provide live technical support and account support to your customers through your Website. Hold online conferences and make your Website a central gathering point for your clients or other interest groups.

29

Use or Benefit:	Examples of Applicability:
Provide tools and resources	Provide customizable maps with driving directions, display a weather forecast, or post stock quotes online. Add tools and calculators to your Website to help your customers do business with you.
Respond instantly to marketplace changes	The marketplace is not a static environment. There is always something new and improved being developed and you must be in real-time control of your business to stay ahead of the competition. Unlike slower, traditional methods of responding to market swings and new developments, your Website is a cutting-edge, *right-now* representation of where your business stands and where it is headed in a changing market.
Round-the-clock marketing	Drip marketing means sending periodic messages to your existing customers to keep them on board. Viral marketing involves customers sending links to interested friends or referrals. Keep up with your customers, and help your customers keep up with your business. Use your Website to manage relationships with people who opt to receive emails from you.
Sell your product or service online	Electronic commerce (e-commerce) adds Point of Sale (POS) capability to a Website. It gives your customers a way to transact business with you efficiently using a variety of payment methods. Customers can place their orders and pay directly online if your site is set up to accept credit cards or bank drafts. Accepting payment for goods and services is not the only use for e-commerce. Non-profit organizations can accept donations, clubs can collect membership dues, etc.

Use or Benefit:	Examples of Applicability:
Share information securely	If you have documents, files, pictures, music, videos or anything else you want to share with employees, members or private groups, store the information on a password protected Web page so it is accessible to the people who need it.
Show portfolios and samples of your work	Portfolios can be a single page or a gallery of still photos. They can also be made into animated slide shows or movies. A Website is a great location for a photographer to place watermarked pictures or proofs for review or to place a portfolio illustrating quality of work. Hair salons, construction companies, lawn care services, weight loss product suppliers, and any other service provider can do the same to show *before* and *after* pictures. Graphics designers can use a site to show their marketing projects and logo designs. In any business where customer trust and confidence is a prerequisite to the sale, your Website can illustrate results representative of your work.
Streamline your administrative processes	Use online forms to collect information from your customers, or have your customers print forms from your Website and submit them to you. Use interactive forms to solicit feedback from your customers, thereby helping you improve service levels. Accept job applications, account applications, or quote requests on your site. Improve communications with your customers by collecting information from forms and creating interest-based mailing lists.

There are few marketing tools as versatile and useful as a Website. If properly marketed, your Internet business presence will become a significant profit center for you, while allowing you to do more with less. That's just smart business.

31

As consumer behavior continues migrating to the Internet, existing marketing methods are doing the same. Phone books, for example, are being published with Internet counterparts around the country for each local area. Empowering customers to look up phone listings on the Web further reduces consumer dependence on the less versatile, printed versions of phone books.

In a similar fashion, community Websites are now appearing online where people can search their local areas for news, movies, social events and more. Daily lifestyle habits are cascading from a physical to a virtual environment, continually eroding the attention that your customers give to previously successful modes of advertisement. Consequently, businesses must rely less on outdated and ineffective marketing methods.

The increasing costs of printed materials will eventually cause traditional business methods to become obsolete. If you have your doubts, let's examine something you have *undoubtedly* used for years: the postage stamp.

Postage costs keep rising. As more banks, utility companies and vendors adapt to the Internet to allow online methods of payment, fewer people are choosing to mail their monthly bills. It's much faster, easier, and cheaper to electronically transfer funds directly from a bank account to a creditor or service provider rather than using a hand-written check.

As a result, there are fewer customers buying postage stamps. The continued decrease in revenues from depressed postage stamp sales makes it necessary to periodically increase the price of postage in order to cover the overhead of processing and delivering the mail. In turn, as postage costs continue to increase, more customers seek alternative ways of paying bills so they turn to online methods. This further compounds the problem of decreasing postage stamp sales, causing yet another increase in stamp prices to offset the downward spiral.

Ultimately, due to the rising costs of postage, not only will all bills be paid online, but all documents will be converted to electronic format and transmitted online. Paper mail traffic will eventually cease to exist as it does today, leaving only markets for packages and freight. The onset of this trend resulting from the Internet paradigm shift is apparent. Many banks and utility companies impose a *convenience fee* for mailing paper statements, thereby encouraging consumers to receive their bills and statements online in lieu of their physical mailbox.

Do *your* bills and statements invite you to pay online? Perhaps now you can see that the trend is irreversible and not just a passing fad.

The signs of the times surround us whether we choose to acknowledge them or not. Ignoring the reality of how the Internet is changing commerce puts your business in a precarious situation. Do not fall prey to the *ostrich syndrome,* sticking your head in the sand and hoping the Internet will go away. It's here to stay. Turning to older ways of marketing in today's Internet economy is to blindly head back to the dark ages at the speed of light. You must *think forward.*

Still, most established businesses rely heavily on *flat* advertisement, meaning ads that are confined to words on a paper page.   Phone books, brochures, business cards, and magazines are all examples of flat ads. In contrast, Websites have depth, sound and motion. Books and ads are made to be read; Websites are made to be *experienced*.

Web pages are interesting and provocative. They cause people to explore, and today's customers anticipate some kind of benefit that they will gain from visiting a Website. This significant detail may explain why businesses *without* Websites are getting ignored by the buying public.

Unlike flat advertising that is paid for solely to deliver value to the business owner, customers feel *entitled* to receive a value from visiting a Website.   In fact, they expect it or they won't come back. If you have no Website, consumers look to companies that can provide the value that you are missing.   The overwhelming benefits that the Internet offers have led to thousands of sites being added to the World Wide Web each day as more businesses capitalize on *high-tech, high-touch* marketing.

Now that you understand more about how a Website can add value to your customers and strengthen your business's bottom line, you must ensure that your online business investment is maximized for exposure and profitability.   To do that, you will need to know some basics about Internet marketing and how to make your business presence readily available for customers to find.

Search Engine Marketing: Important?

Are You Lost in the Shuffle?

Once you decide to establish a Website, you should ensure that your site is designed to be found on Internet *search engines* so your new online investment isn't lost in the shuffle among the growing millions of other Websites. The process to improve your site's chances of being found is called Search Engine Optimization, and it is an essential part of a successful Web presence.

To illustrate, I have a couple of very important questions for you. First, if you visit a search engine (for example, Google.com) and submit a search for your business, your products, or your services in your local area, does your business show up? Whose does?

If you did a search to find your own company and someone else's showed up, then you were successful in finding *your competition*. Now, here's another very important question— one with an answer that might eventually "break your bank account":

> If you looked online for your business but ended up finding your *competition* instead, where are your customers or clients going when *they* try to find you online?

You probably don't like the answer.

Every business owner wants the Number One spot on the search engine listings for a given set of keyword selections. Unfortunately, no one can realistically promise you the Number One spot for any particular

35

word in the way your site naturally appears in a search. It is just not possible to make such a guarantee. Otherwise, everyone who pays to optimize their site would be assured the Number One spot, and it's not logical that more than one Website could hold that position. So beware of empty promises and undeliverable guarantees in your search for a Web solution.

Not all Websites are created equal. In fact, if you are unfamiliar with owning a Website, you may be interested to learn that relatively few sites are actually able to be found by customers on the search engines. Now ask yourself this: what good is your Website if nobody can find it? Would you ever buy a billboard advertisement that faces *away* from traffic? Of course not! It just wouldn't make sense. Believe it or not, though, many business owners are lured into doing *exactly* that with their Website. Having a professional *looking* Website is only part of your online solution. Successfully promoting and marketing it is another part of the equation.

Basic Websites are relatively easy to build. There are plenty of programs and packages for sale that allow you to build your site without any programming experience, and there are many business owners who try to cut costs by having someone they know build a "free" site for them.

It is perfectly understandable and just good business sense to cut costs where you can. Also, it is very difficult to argue with "free", but how much will a "free" site end up costing you in the long run?

When it comes to Websites, what you see isn't always what you get. What you save up front can end up costing you thousands of dollars more in hidden costs, wasted expense, and opportunity costs. For a moment, let's revisit the billboard analogy mentioned earlier in this section.

If the typical billboard advertisement costs $5000, and if I were to offer it to you at the great *price* of only $2500, would you be interested? Oh, but there's one little drawback—the billboard is behind some trees, and it is facing away from the road so no one can see it. But the price is right— at a 50% discount, aren't you interested? No? Why not?

Okay, let's save you even *more* money on the deal. I'll arbitrarily drop the price even further to $1000 for that same billboard. Now, for a billboard (facing away from traffic), what do you think about that—a $4000 savings off of regular pricing? Would you pay for it?

Let's get ridiculously affordable. What if I drop the price to under $500 and make it twice normal size? I'll even shine some spotlights on it for you. How about now? Would you pay for it, knowing that it will never be seen by anyone? Of course not!

You can probably see where we're going with this. No matter how cheap I make the *price* of that billboard, you would be foolish to buy it because it would have no *value*. Why not? Well, no matter how big it is, how pretty it is, or how many bells & whistles it's equipped with, it simply wouldn't meet your needs if no one can see it. Don't make that mistake with your Website!

37

Don't be "penny wise but pound foolish" when it comes to establishing your business online. If you opt to get a cheap, or even a free solution, but no one can find you on the Internet, then you don't have a solution at all! Consequently, every dollar you spend on hosting is wasted, and every customer you lose to your competition becomes an opportunity cost. Normally the value of *free* is *zero*. However, a *free* site that isn't effective can have the same effect as not having one at all. In other words, in the case of your Website, *free* can eventually cost you your business.

Okay, enough doom and gloom for now. It is not my intent to shake your confidence, and I'm not trying to employ scare tactics to get you to pay more than you want to for a Website. There are several cost effective solutions available to you that will work within even the slimmest of budgets. You need to be aware, however, that "cheap" and "free" can actually be very costly if you don't exercise due diligence in obtaining a solution that meets your needs.

What goes *into* your Website can be even more important than what goes *onto* your Website. When you set out to establish your affordable online solution, be sure that your site is optimized so your customers can find you. Websites can be optimized for local searches or national searches depending on your target audience. Ensure that the Website solution provider or build-it-yourself software you end up using is equipped and qualified to support effective Search Engine Optimization.

Confirm that your Website hosting provider equips your site with tools that enable you to view reports of your site's traffic, so you can track the effectiveness of your marketing efforts. You need more than just a "hit counter" that some companies will try to sell you. Use a hosting and management package that includes meaningful information such as peak usage times, sources of traffic, visits listed by time and date, keywords people use to find you and more.

Statistics vary, but to emphasize the importance of Search Engine Optimization, commonly called *SEO*, people use the Internet approximately fifteen to one (15:1) over the phone book and other sources of consumer research. That's an increase from an estimated 7:1 just a few years ago. The trend is obvious: the Internet is here to stay, and if people can't find your business on it, you're losing money at an ever-increasing rate as more consumers join the ranks of online shoppers. Think about it this way: if you don't have a Website, those are *your* customers that you are losing.

Whether you already have a Website or are just now taking the first steps to get one, be sure that your Website is focused on promoting your company effectively. Consider how important it is that your online presence includes content, tools, features, and benefits that empower you to manage your business and your customers on the Internet. It is important that your customers can find what they want quickly and easily.

Businesses typically place phone book ads in just one or two categories due to advertising costs, so consumers must try to figure out what heading to look under when they thumb through hundreds of pages. It's so much easier for them to type in what they want on a search engine, click a button, and have their exact matches served to them on the screen. Consumers aren't *lazy;* they're *smart.* They recognize that search engines are much more efficient than any other method of doing research.

Now, let's think about this: how many people use computers at work? Millions—and at home? Millions more. Today, people work online, bank online, check mail online, make friends and date online, and more. Virtually every aspect of our culture has an Internet counterpart. While people do their daily tasks and errands online, check the news and weather, and such, why not shop, too? And they do. Online shopping has become an increasingly integral part of our society, exceeding $130 billion in sales in 2007 alone. Why? Because shopping over the Internet is so easy and convenient.

Many business owners have the misconception that a phone book ad, billboard, radio broadcast or other type of promotion is adequate for driving customers to their business. True, those methods *help* to capture customers' attention, but once the customer hears or reads the advertisement, their next question is often, "What's your Web address?"

If you do not have a Website and your customers frequently ask what your Web address is, it's a warning sign that they are looking online for the product or service that you provide. If you have a Website, it is a buying sign. Dismissing the question with, "We don't have one." sends the message that you aren't up with the times and aren't interested in serving your customers' needs. In turn, you have just sent them to your competition.

Let's look a little deeper into why a Website makes sense for your business.

You own a business (or manage a business or in some other way are a decision-maker for a business). Let's say, for illustration purposes, that it's a pet store. Suppose you sell pets, pet supplies, and offer a typical variety of pet-related services like grooming, boarding, and veterinary services. Under which category do you place your phone book ad?

Pets? Pet Supplies? Kennels? Grooming? Or perhaps, veterinarians? Well, advertising dollars are scarce, and at hundreds or thousands of dollars per ad each month, you will have some tough decisions to make. You will have to guess where your customers will look for you the most, just as your customers will have to guess where to find you. After all, you want to pick the one or two categories that will yield the biggest return on your advertising dollar, right? When you do so, it is to the exclusion of promoting your other products and services.

But what if you could be listed in *all* of the categories of products and services that you provide? And instead of spending hundreds or thousands of dollars each month *hoping* to attract customers with printed phone book ads (that can only be updated once a year), or broadcast ads that you *hope* will reach your target audience, what if you could pay once for a Website and then pay only a nominal monthly hosting fee? If the costs are less and the results are better, wouldn't it make sense for your business to consider the Website option?

A Website can be optimized for search engines and equipped with tools such that your customers can find you by name or by any of the categories, manufacturers, or other keywords that you define. Additionally, it can be updated as often as necessary to keep up with changes, new products, and more. Unlike other advertising, you will know how many people saw your ad, what words they used to find it, and how long they took to read it. There will be no more guessing and hoping when it comes to the effectiveness of your marketing dollars.

Remember, your Website is more than a paid-for advertisement. It is a tool that adds value to your customer's shopping experience while simultaneously adding value to your business. Whereas you want your customers to find you online, *they want to find you, too*, especially if they receive some kind of benefit in doing so. Being *findable* on the Internet is not a simple process, but in the hands of a competent Internet marketing company that specializes in promoting Websites, you should have little difficulty achieving favorable results in a reasonable period of time.

Assuming that the person or company that markets your site is experienced and knowledgeable in Search Engine Marketing (SEM), the results you achieve are dependent on three basic elements: budget, strategy, and effort. Although all three elements are necessary, none of the three needs to be excessive. For instance, you do not need a robust budget for good results in many cases, and a little extra effort on your part can usually offset the limitations of a tight budget. Likewise, if time is a challenge and you are not able to put the requisite amount of effort into marketing your business yourself, a little extra money put towards marketing with a competent SEO company can offset your time constraints by delivering the desired results.

No matter who provides your Web solution, it is important that you know how effective your promotions and advertisements are. It's important that your site can be updated in a timely manner. It's important that your site is focused around your customers' needs. Most importantly, your customers must be able to *find* your site through your effective marketing and search engine listings.

Points to ponder for effective Search Engine Optimization and Marketing (SEO/SEM):

- You must distinguish between the *price* of your site and the *value* it delivers. Price and value are different.

- A "Free" site can be costly in the long-run if it is poorly built and does not deliver results.

- Paying for effective SEO from an experienced professional is worth the money.

- People must be able to find your site on the Internet or your site is a wasted expense.

- More people use and respond to the Internet to find products and services than the phone book.

- Internet advertisement is more affordable and more versatile than ads in the phone book.

- You can update your Website faster and more frequently than phone book or other printed ads.

- E-commerce sales continue to increase about 25% each year, indicating a momentous shift in consumer spending habits.

Usability: Helpful Website or Nuisance?

Do You Have a *Sticky* Website?

Aiming to be found on the first page of search results may be your goal, but it can take time to get there. Plus, there is more to a successful Website solution than solely achieving a prominent search engine ranking. Once your customers find you online, you will need to provide them with an incentive to *stay* on your site and to come back—so you *keep* them as customers.

Finding and using the right keywords make up only a fraction of your Website's success. Consumers are very fickle and choosy on the Internet. If they find you through a search engine but they don't like your site or can't find what they need right away, their next action is to click the *Back* button of their Web browser and move on to the next listing (even if your search engine ranking *is* number one).

Herein is one of the biggest challenges of the average Web developer. Your Website may have a clean and professional appearance, but from a navigational or functional standpoint, it may not serve the needs of your customers. Of course it's possible that the site may be aesthetically unappealing as well, especially if it was created without considering the *marketing* aspects of good Web design.

The term that encompasses layout, marketing, navigation, and functionality considerations together is *Usability*. Usability is an often-overlooked facet to a Website. It is intangible, perceptional, and also somewhat subjective. Most software packages that you buy in a store go through a process called *beta-testing* prior to a final release to the public. Beta-testing allows the manufacturer to obtain feedback from people who will use the software, apart from the people who developed it. Testing a Website in the same fashion is not only important—it is *essential*.

Why, then, is usability testing so rare in Web design? Many Web designers are not complete Internet solutions providers. Some are basically Internet artists, paid to put attractive looking pages together like a graphics designer would put together a brochure. Although they may be competent designing the appearance and basic mechanics of a Website from a visual standpoint, they may not be experienced in testing a site from a user's perspective.

Designing a Website without an independent usability test equates to the inefficiencies of writers proofreading their own work. To be effective in considering usability, a second (or third, etc.) set of eyes is a necessity.

What is the impact of *not* incorporating a usability review into your Website solution? Short answer: twelve seconds. Twelve seconds is the estimated amount of useful consciousness that people devote to a Website when they visit it via the search engines. After twelve seconds of not finding what they want, they click the *Back* button. After twelve seconds of frustration, they choose the next site on the list of dozens, hundreds or thousands of your competitors. Twelve seconds is all you have to make your first and (often) only impression before you lose a potential customer *forever*.

Let's look at it another way: you have twelve seconds to make a return on your investment. Test the theory. Time yourself the next time you search for a product or service on the Internet. How long does it take you to move on to the next site on the list?

The tendency for Internet users to stay on a site rather than shift to another in short order is a measure of *stickiness*. If the site is quickly abandoned by a visitor, it *isn't* sticky. If it captures their attention and they stay (and possibly bookmark it in their *favorites* selections), it *is* sticky.

In light of that, you may agree that the seemingly trivial detail of usability takes on a much more profound impact if it is ignored. Therefore, reconsider having the neighbor kid throw something together for "free." The brother-neighbor-uncle-coworker-friend who tells you that they'll do you a favor by putting together a free site has the best of intentions but generally won't produce worthwhile results.

I am not suggesting that you discard all offers for a free Website from would-be helpful family, friends or associates. There are times when such an option may meet your needs perfectly. My advice, however, is to ask questions—a lot of questions—of the person or company being considered for the job.

As with every industry, the Website world has its jargon plus its fair share of abbreviations and acronyms. To the uninitiated, Website and programming lingo just seems like a random array of letters and gobbledygook. People in the industry talk in cryptic terms, using letters like HTML to stand for the programming language of Hypertext Markup

Language, which in itself sounds difficult and would have no meaning to a non-tech person.

Web people need to know such details, but as a business owner, you *don't*. The point, here, is that knowing HTML, XML, PHP, or any "alphabet soup" programming languages of Web design doesn't necessarily qualify someone to create an *effective, sticky* online presence.

Even the aspiring new graduate with a Web design diploma from a local technical school may not be thinking of usability elements when he or she creates a Website for your business. New graduates and inexperienced programmers have a steep learning curve in today's competitive Web design market. In school they learn the valuable and necessary information that most of us find intimidating if we're not technical people. When your business is concerned, it is better to work with proven experience rather than textbook theory. Be sure your Website developer has the right experience.

Would you want your dream home to be the first real-life project of a newly graduated architect, or would you prefer to invest a bit more money in the skills of a seasoned professional? Comparatively, don't become the guinea pig that pays for a well-intentioned student's learning curve at the expense of your business or livelihood.

In the event you are considering an out-of-the box program from a retail store to help you create your own site, you may need to make significant changes to the templates that come as part of the package in order to meet your business's needs. Be sure you do your due diligence and take the time to make your Website a useful labor of love, rather than a throw-together picture puzzle. It's okay to be ambitious about creating your own Web presence, but be realistic at the same time. You want the end result to be an attraction to your customers, not a turnoff.

To be sticky, your site needs more than the one-size-fits-none, "cookie cutter" look and feel resulting from using many of the do-it-yourself software packages. Likewise, before committing your time and money to allow a developer to put ideas together for your Website, be sure to know what criteria they consider for usability factors. Interview the developer so you have confidence that your investment will pay for itself by creating loyal, repeat customers online. If the developer can't explain the features and benefits of the site pertinent to your customers and your business, it's best to keep looking.

To put usability factors in perspective, do the following as an exercise. Visit your favorite search engine and do a search for one or two keywords that relate to your business. Visit two or three of the Websites that result from each keyword search, making notes of what you like or dislike about each site. Once you have a list of pros and cons of the sites you visited, consider what might fix the elements that you dislike.

As you reviewed each site in the exercise above, you assumed the role of *Website user*, rather than *Website owner*. The sites were not yours, so you were able to evaluate each one objectively. Use your list of likes and dislikes from the exercise to ensure your preferences are included in the design when your Website is built. If you already have a site, you can compare your notes to what you currently have, and you will have suggestions to give to your Website developer for anything that must be refurbished.

When you are browsing for something on the Internet, get into the practice of writing down anything positive or negative that you find noteworthy. As you continue to browse the Web as a consumer, compare your notes with the look and feel of your own site to determine what should stay and what should go.

Your site will continually improve with subtle changes that enhance usability. Meanwhile, search engines tend to favor Websites with fresh content, so the updates you make to your site may also contribute to better search engine placement over time.

Regardless of how involved you become with your Website's usability, it is worthwhile to have someone with relevant experience evaluate the design of your site. If you have an existing Website and enjoy a productive relationship with your current Web developer who does not have the resources to provide you with an independent usability review, have an experienced third-party Web professional review your site and provide a summary of recommendations for your Web developer to implement.

Some of the underlying design considerations may not be intuitive, and a usability review may provide recommendations which contradict some of your own ideas for improvement. In such cases, be sure that the conflicting suggestions are fully explained to you, and then make the decision that you are most comfortable with in representing your business online.

Remember, it's *your* business. A usability report is intended to help you make informed decisions, not make you relinquish control of your Website. Make your twelve seconds count.

Things to remember about Website Usability:

⌐ Visitors judge your business by your Website's ease-of-use.

⌐ If you want your customers to re-visit your site, it must be built with Usability in mind.

⌐ You have 12 seconds to make a positive impression on your Website visitors before they look elsewhere.

<u>Piecing Together The Website Triangle</u>

Does Your Solution Have All of the Points?

As you can surmise, a successful Website must include the three elements of design, search engine optimization, and usability. Each of these key components serves a specific purpose in an effective online solution and together they make up *The Website Triangle*.

The Website Triangle™

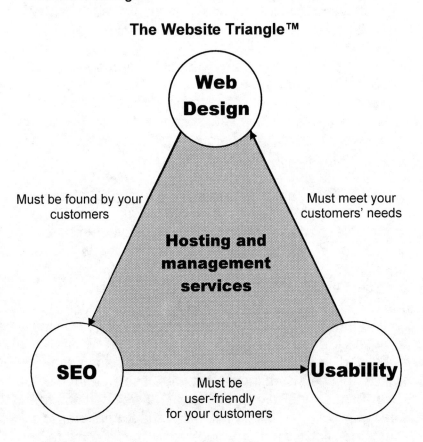

At the apex of the Triangle, Web design represents the physical code (programming) that comprises the layout and features of your site. You can think of it as the visible site itself. The site design is your business's presence on the Internet. Without the design programming, there is no Website.

The left leg of the Triangle illustrates the need for your customers to be able to *find* your Website, leading us to the second point of The Website Triangle, Search Engine Optimization (SEO). In actuality, SEO is part programming and part marketing. Without it, your site is ineffective— just a figurative *billboard facing away from traffic.*

The base leg of the Triangle represents the progression from being found on the Internet via search engines to captivating your customers' attention with your Website's appeal. This leads to the user-friendliness of your site, or as we have discussed, usability optimization.

This third point, usability, includes layout considerations but is mainly focused around the intangible aspects of making your customers feel comfortable during their visit. Usability is about meeting their needs. Aesthetics, navigation simplicity, intuitiveness, and *site depth* make up usability.

Site depth involves the number of pages that a visitor must click through to get deep enough into the site so they find what they want. The fewer pages that it takes to find what they want, the easier and more user-friendly the site is to them. A well-constructed site with solid usability maximizes the potential that a customer finds what they look for within the average twelve seconds of attention they give it.

Completing the Triangle, the third leg brings your customers back to your physical site as repeat visitors, ensuring *stickiness.* If your site is sticky, it remains their first choice when they surf the Internet to shop and do research for what you sell. A successfully completed Website Triangle leads to loyal customers, your site being bookmarked, links to your site from other Websites, and word-of-mouth referral traffic online.

There is one more element of The Website Triangle that underlies your entire online solution, and that is the service that hosts your site. Your Website's hosting is irrelevant to your customers, but it is an integral part of your solution from a management and administration standpoint. It can be as plain and simple as monthly rented space on a Web server (computer) in someone's garage, to very elaborate platforms which provide technical services, analysis tools, and software applications. Since it is behind the scenes, it makes up the background of The Website Triangle.

If any piece of The Website Triangle is missing or broken, you don't have a complete online solution. Additionally, your Website presence is only as strong as the weakest link in the Triangle, so you must take measures to continually improve each element for the long-term success of your business.

Visualizing The Website Triangle will help you address your questions with a Web developer and focus on what is important. Stay on track and avoid the distraction of extra bells and whistles that you do not need. If a particular provider does not offer one or more aspects of The Website Triangle and they cannot refer you to a specialized company that addresses those aspects, then it is to your advantage to take your business elsewhere.

The Website Triangle makes it easy to remember:

The key components to your Website solution involve site design, SEO, usability and hosting.

The Website Triangle provides you with a memory aid to focus your questions related to Website solutions.

Section Two: Your Options

Topics Covered:

Know Your Options

Build-It-Yourself Solutions

Traditional Website Developers

Turnkey Solutions

and

Website Hosting

Transition to the Web

If you own a brick-and-mortar store or a service business without a storefront, think of a Website as the expansion of your traditional business to give you a physical presence on the Internet.

Know Your Options

With So Many Choices, What's Right for YOU?

Since you are still reading, I assume that you understand the value that an effective Web presence offers your business. Congratulations! There are many business owners and organizational leaders who choose to dismiss the notion of doing business online even after understanding the concepts in the preceding pages.

Many of those who resist getting a Website simply hope that a gradual economic downturn is merely a temporary slip in profitability. However, as consumers and businesses continue transitioning to the Internet, the ongoing financial slide of companies *without* Websites is resulting in their continued, downward spirals terminating in bankruptcies.

A common challenge that business owners face is overcoming fear of the Internet. A second challenge is seeing how spending a little capital on a Web solution can change their negative economic trend into profitable growth. If the Website-less business is losing money, the business owner is typically unreceptive to spending *more* money on technology that he or she finds intimidating. Instead, that business owner is inclined to conserve dollars during times of severe financial scrutiny and ultimately ends up buying a "Going Out of Business" sign rather than a Website.

Now that you understand the necessity of an effective Website, what should you do to establish one? There are a number of ways to get started, but we can group them into three general categories: self-built, traditional Web development, and turnkey packages. Each has distinct advantages and disadvantages associated with functionality, usability, and costs. There is no right or wrong answer regarding which method you should use to set up your Website.

The question you need to answer is *which best fits your business's unique needs?* The remainder of this section discusses the details regarding each type of Web solution so you can make an informed decision.

Factors to consider in order to move forward:

Being intimidated by technology can cause analysis paralysis in making a decision.

Resistance to spending more money when you're losing money is normal, but it can aggravate your situation.

You have three options in getting started: self-built, turnkey, or traditional design.

You need to know the advantages, disadvantages, costs, and other details about each option.

The Build-It-Yourself Solution

If money is scarce but time is no factor, you may want to consider building your own Website. Realize, up front, that to do it right will require several days, weeks, or months of work, plus you will need to augment the Website design with the other two points in The Website Triangle: search engine optimization and usability considerations. If you are resourceful, you can find programs and services a-la-carte to make a build-it-yourself solution work at a fraction of typical development costs.

Let's first look at where people fail with this approach so we can avoid the common pitfalls. You must be realistic with your expectations. After you do your due diligence in considering your business's needs, you will be prepared to decide whether or not you should try to build your site yourself.

Being thrifty makes good sense for some things, but too many cost-conscious business owners buy a do-it-yourself program, pick a template, add some text and pictures, and then think that they have a site that will make a difference in their businesses—or they may have "the neighbor kid" do it for a quick few bucks. If only they would save their money!

Building a Website yourself can be cost-effective, but it is also a laborious process. On the positive side, it can be a labor of love and a lot of fun to exert your creativity. If you do it right, you'll have satisfaction and a claim to originality. Like so many things in life, you will get out of it what you put into it.

If you are a programmer and know how to write in Hypertext Markup Language (HTML), you're off to a good start. There are several other Web design languages that can be used to build a Website, but learning how to program in HTML or other Website development languages is technical and beyond the scope of this book.

On the likely chance that you are *not* a programmer, there are several off-the-shelf software packages that you can purchase to help you build your own site. A casual stroll through the software aisle at your local computer mega-store or neighborhood department store will yield half a dozen titles or more. Programs such as Adobe® GoLive®, Adobe® Dreamweaver®, and Microsoft® FrontPage® are very powerful and well-suited for creating your own Web presence. Of course, you must shop around and determine which software package offers the features that will best meet your needs.

Programs that allow you to build your own site typically offer pre-defined templates to showcase the look and feel of your Web presence. Doing so saves you the trouble of learning how to design buttons, backgrounds, banners, borders, and headers for your Website.

Most of the template designs have blank spaces set aside in the layouts to allow you to enter text and pictures so you can finish the site yourself in a relatively short period of time. The time consuming part of using an off-the-shelf program is actually learning how to use the software and then tailoring the look and feel so that it does not appear to be from a generic template.

From a usability standpoint, your customers will likely be unimpressed with a "cookie cutter," one-size-fits-none look that stems from simply placing words and images into a template. You will need to take the time to finesse your Website's look and feel to make it appealing and effective.

The beautiful part about using a do-it-yourself program is that the program actually creates the HTML script while you edit the site's appearance with simple drag-and-drop, cut-and-paste, and point-and-click actions around the screen.

Do-it-yourself programs make it simple and easy to create forms, add content, and preview your work before you commit it to the Internet. You can make additional changes to your Website with the program as often as you want and then update your site on the hosting service that you use.

Several third-party Websites on the Internet provide free (or low cost) portions of HTML and other types of programming code that you can copy and paste into your own Web design to add features and functionality.

Two such sites among my personal favorites are _www.javascriptsource.com_ and _www.dynamicdrive.com_. These sites provide specific instructions on how to copy and paste special effects, calculators, and other applications into your own Website to make your site more eye-catching, user-friendly, and interactive.

Once you have created your initial Website layout and changed it to suit your needs, you will need to determine the keywords that you expect your customers to use to find your business online. Remember, optimizing your site for the search engines is an important part of any online solution. It will take a good bit of time and effort to achieve the search engine placement that you want, but you should be able to achieve the desired results through consistency and persistence.

We discuss keywords and search engine criteria later in this book to help you optimize your Website, but to do the search engine optimization (SEO) correctly without any negative consequences to your site's placement, you should find an SEO expert if you aren't one yourself.

After determining keywords, optimizing your site, and adjusting your text to flow the way you want it to, your remaining task to finish your own online solution is to review your site for completeness, intactness, and intuitiveness.

Does your site do everything you want it to do? Does it contain any broken links or unlinked pages? Can people find what they want and navigate your site without any problem? This step in creating your own Web solution is best made with the help of a friend or person who will lend a critical eye to find the details that you have overlooked.

As you put your ideas together, ask for candid feedback on ways to improve your design. Also double check spelling, grammar, and punctuation.

The following paragraph is an example illustrating why it is so important to have someone else evaluate your site for correctness, completeness, and other usability considerations:

> Jsut as its esay to figrue out waht tihs snetence is saiyng, yuor brian wlil oevrlook deatils in yuor web desgin taht yuo wlil not detcet. It may eevn be dificlut for anthoer pesron to see a mistkae, but its mroe liekly taht tehy wlil tahn yuo wlil, sicne yuo are the auhtor of yuor own matreial.

You may have had to read the preceding paragraph a bit slower to absorb it, but you probably found it understandable.   Now, go back and count the misspelled words. How many were there? Are you sure? You may need to count them again.

The answer: there are 38 mistakes in that one short paragraph (including the missing apostrophes in the word "it's").   But your brain finds the compromise between what is *written* and what is *meant* when groups of words are used together in context. The end result is that you read right through the mistakes and your eyes become desensitized to the errors. In part, this explains why it is so hard to proofread your own work; your brain already knows what you meant when you wrote the material the first time, so your mistakes become invisible to yourself.

In a similar fashion, your Website visitors may experience difficulty finding their way around a site that is unedited. Sure, it's easy for you to find your way around your own site; you created it. You know where you planned to go, and you put pages, links, and buttons in place accordingly. Your customers can't read your mind, though. So finding an impartial, objective, and otherwise disinterested person to provide you with meaningful, constructive criticism will help make your site much more user-friendly. Do not be offended by their candid observations. Their feedback will help your business succeed online. Remember, ultimately your site is for your customers' use, not just your own.

Revise your Website to encompass the relevant changes. These final changes will help you complete your site to a point that is easy to maintain moving forward. As you will learn later in this book, it's important to make minor updates to your site on an occasional basis, but after your first major usability review, subsequent changes to your site will involve much less time than what you initially must invest.

Considerations for a do-it-yourself Website:

👍   It is cheaper and gives you more control than working through a traditional design company.

👍   You have direct access to all of your information and can be creative with your own ideas.

👎   It can be time consuming and tedious to learn the software and create your site's content.

👎   Shopping for hosting, features, and services can be inconvenient and may result in compatibility issues between service providers.

☠   Do not expect to achieve top-tier search engine results by trying to optimize your own site without SEO experience.

☺   If you build your own Website, ask people for unbiased opinions and suggestions so you can improve it.

The Traditional Website Developer

The role of a traditional Website developer is to provide your business with a functional Web presence on the Internet. Developers usually work on an hourly basis plus charge an initial development fee to put together ideas that you evaluate and approve. Within the scope of a Website project, your Web design takes shape in phases, each phase being a billable interval for work completed to that point. In this way, the Website developer is assured that they are paid for work they perform, while you can be assured that the work being done meets your expectations.

The development fee is customarily non-refundable, but in many cases it may be applied towards the first billable checkpoint. Understandably, the traditional development company must still pay its programmers whether or not you like the initial ideas that they put together. If you decide to take your business elsewhere, the developer is still able to cover their overhead expenses from the fee collected.

The upside to working with a traditional developer is that you *should* eventually end up with exactly what you want, and the Website can be equipped with elaborate tools and services dovetailed into the design. Compare this to the do-it-yourself option where you may need to look for multiple sources and test compatibility to create the desired results. If your business needs to have a Website that combines intricate databases, elaborate interactivity between site visitors and their business accounts, customized quotes and estimates computed from online forms, multimedia such as live (streaming) audio and video, etc, then using a traditional developer is likely the right path to pursue. Large corporations whose Web solutions must interact with Websites from other companies or companies that require a significant amount of information processing on the Internet are also limited to working with a traditional developer. The results are predictably better if one development company integrates all of the necessary design factors into a Website built "under one roof, from the ground up."

The downside to the traditional developer approach is indisputably *costs*. Because most traditional developers work on an a-la-carte basis plus hourly rates, there is plenty of room to run up a bill. The uninitiated business owner who shops for a Website will often view the final bill as being laced with a bunch of "hidden" costs and "nickel and dime" fees. In reality there is a lot more to a site than what is displayed on the screen. It all takes time to build, and time costs money. Although reputable developers' bills may seem high, they've *earned* the money that they charge.

Every Website is different. When a developer begins work on a site, they have a picture in mind for the end result. Over time, the picture changes shape based on what you, the customer, convey to your developer about what you like and dislike. Meanwhile, as the picture is taking shape into multiple Web pages, online applications, calculators, text, images and more, the Web developer must be working towards the balance between aesthetics and functionality. Every time you adjust something at a billable checkpoint, there is rework involved on the developer's end.

For example, if an unplanned page is added (or one is deleted) midway through a project, the navigation buttons and menus on every existing page must be redone to accommodate the change. In a Website, all of the pages are interconnected, involving substantial time to make a seemingly quick change.

The a-la-carte pricing generally covers the functionality issues with Web design, while the hourly fees tend to cover time-related costs with work and rework. When it is done, a well-conceived Website can have a phenomenal, positive impact on your business, but the associated development costs can be substantial. Be prepared that a traditional developer may provide you with the best results, but the costs can add up quickly if you continually change the design, or if you are a person who will "know what you want when you see it."

The timeliness of making updates to your site is another consideration when working with Web developers. Based on the workload of a traditional development company, you may or may not be able to make changes to your site in a timeframe that meets your needs. Again, work involves hourly fees, and other customers have changes to make as well. Your site will fall somewhere in the pecking order.

For an additional fee, you may be able to prioritize your work ahead of other customers on an urgency basis. Whether you pay regular or priority rates to get the work done, hourly fees for routine updates can become excessive if you work in an industry that demands frequent changes to your site. If you believe your business will need multiple changes each month to your Website and if you opt to get a

Website through a traditional developer, find one who will offer you a prorated rate based on time actually spent, versus one who charges "per hour or any part thereof." Better yet, work with a developer who adds content management tools to your site so you can change it yourself.

When you set out to find a qualified Web development company, look beyond the front reception room. Don't settle for a faceless name in the phone book. Insist on seeing a sample of the developer's work prior to making a commitment. Established, reputable developers will have a portfolio of Websites to illustrate the quality of their work. I recommend that you visit live sites that they have produced so you can see animations, click on navigation links, and get a sense of layout, balance, and how long it takes pages to load. In other words, visiting a live site will allow you to critique usability issues that you cannot glean from viewing a still-shot picture of a Web page.

Remember, a Website's appearance is only one element of The Website Triangle, so shop around for a development firm that encompasses the other elements of the Triangle into their solutions. This is where we must make the distinction between a *Website development company* and a complete *solutions provider.* In your research, you will find that many design companies offer Websites, but the sites may not be optimized for the search engines or evaluated for navigation and usability.

A *developer* simply designs Websites. *A solutions provider* includes all of the elements in The Website Triangle as a package. Pricing of your Web presence will reflect the services offered, accordingly. Unless a specific distinction is made, this book refers to Web developers and solution providers interchangeably.

The "college kid next door" or the amateur freelance programmer who passes him or herself off as a Web developer may be proficient at making a Web page but certainly is *not* an Internet solutions provider. In fact, if you pay an individual developer to create a Website for you, you might be surprised to learn that he or she may use one of the do-it-yourself programs described in the previous section to build your site.

That's not a problem if you are satisfied with the end result, but be sure you are not paying thousands of dollars for a basic template, only to end up with a homemade look and feel that doesn't meet your needs. What software do they use to create Websites? Ask the question. If you decide to use a traditional Web developer, you should expect to end up with a professional, high-end product that will likely have a bill commensurate with the quality of work performed.

If you choose to work with a freelance Web developer rather than a complete solutions provider, you should still expect to be charged a fair price for the site and services you receive. Just realize that you will likely need to look elsewhere for someone to optimize your site and adjust it for usability. Since you will probably be paying a-la-carte for those services anyway, your choice is more a matter of convenience than competence. A complete solutions provider simply does it all as one-stop shopping.

As a footnote to the distinction between solution providers and Web developers, some Internet solution providers establish strategic partnerships with specialized companies to provide search engine optimization and usability reviews, while other providers do all of the work in-house. Either way is fine, so long as the usability reviews done in-house are being performed by different people than those who created your site.

Remember that initial cost estimates are little more than guesses because the scope of your Website will change as progress is made on the project. A traditional developer is probably the best option to choose if you have a stout budget, little time for establishing or maintaining your Web presence, and service requirements that are elaborate enough that a do-it-yourself option isn't feasible to meet your needs.

Considerations in using a Traditional Designer:

The final product should be a professional look that is exactly to your specifications.

You don't need to be a Web expert or learn how to do anything technical.

The Website development and subsequent updates can be expensive or take longer than you would like.

Beware of amateurs posing as professionals, or you may end up paying traditional developer prices for a do-it-yourself look.

Ask to see a portfolio of samples to verify quality of work and experience.

Get a detailed consultation before committing to do business with a developer.

The Turnkey Solution

If time and money are limited, there is yet another option to equip your business with an online solution. A major paradigm shift has occurred within the Website market, introducing *turnkey solutions* that provide specialty services and tools while allowing you to control your content at a significant cost and time savings. Turnkey solutions are a hybrid between the do-it-yourself option and a traditional design.

What does *turnkey* mean in terms of Websites, and how do turnkey solutions represent a change in the Website industry? Let's explore. To get an appreciation for the turnkey concept, we will use an analogous situation with the movie industry.

Years ago, animated movies were created by hand-drawing the scenes frame by frame, and each frame was played sequentially through a projector. The resulting animation was much like an old-style flip book. Animated movies were two-dimensional "flat" moving pictures that sometimes lacked smooth, fluid motion. The process to create such a movie was time-intensive and laborious, prone to mistakes and inconsistencies resulting from human error.

In movie-making today, computers make it possible to generate realistic, three-dimensional animated characters that are lifelike in appearance, lighting, shading, and motion. Full length movies are created in a fraction of the time by fewer people. It is done through automation. The animation industry experienced a paradigm shift from people creating animation to computers creating animation.

Comparably, today we have computer programs that create entire Websites rather than relying on programmers to do the development work by hand. Automation is faster, cheaper, and more precise than human labor, so it is often more cost effective to consider an automated, or turnkey Website design. Common features or characteristics from one site to another can be pre-assembled by the computer, requiring little to no human intervention. By combining the power of word processing, information analysis, and interactive forms, turnkey solution companies are able to include basic tools that allow non-technical people to easily make changes to their Websites.

A turnkey solution involves automatically creating your own Website by *using software to create software*. The actual work is done by the computer so you do not have to be a programmer, and it is not a do-it-yourself from scratch design project in which you need to learn how to install and use a program. A turnkey solution might possibly have everything a small to medium-size business needs for doing business on the Internet.

Turnkey solutions allow you to create your own Website by using simple actions such as point-and-click, drag-and-drop, and cut-and-paste, similar to a do-it-yourself Website. However, turnkey sites usually come complete with customizable pictures, text, tools, calculators, and services relevant to your type of business. They differ from the do-it-yourself templates discussed earlier because content management tools, hosting, search engine optimization tools, and more are all included as a package. There is no need to mix and match from multiple providers. It is one-stop shopping. For small to medium-size businesses, there are multiple advantages to using a turnkey solution and comparatively few drawbacks.

One of the biggest advantages is price. For the tools, services, and professional appearance that you would typically expect to pay $5000 to $7000 to a traditional developer, you can find an approximately equivalent turnkey package for a fraction of the price. The tradeoff? Basically, *time*. Would it be worth it if you could save $4000 or so off the price of a Website and also save hundreds of dollars in the costs of ongoing changes to the site in exchange for being able to maintain the Website yourself? If so, then the turnkey solution may be right for you.

If you think that you might be interested in using a turnkey solution, take the time to write down a list of features, benefits, and tools that you would find important. Then find a turnkey Website solution that best matches those requirements.

Once you find a good match between form, fit, and function, take a look at the service level that you can expect with that solution. Are you on your own? Or, do you have technical support available to help you manage your Website? If you have access to technical support, is it free or do you have to pay for it per instance? Is the technical support limited to phone usage, or does the technical support staff have the ability to interact with you online?

Ask questions. Visit Websites of various turnkey providers and read through their features, benefits, and articles that relate to their particular packages.

There is another advantage to the turnkey concept that has nothing to do with ease of use or cost savings. It is *self-reliance*.

The typical Web developer has a production schedule. They allocate time and resources to the projects that are on their calendar, much like any manager would prioritize tasks to run a business. When using a traditional developer, you may find that their production schedule does not accommodate emergent changes to your Website.

Most Website solution companies will do everything they can to meet your needs, but realize that an impromptu shift in their workload might translate to doing your work at premium rates due to overtime that they have to pay their programmers.

In comparison, most turnkey packages provide enough tools and controls to allow you to make your own changes on a real-time basis, allowing you to handle any emergent requirements yourself. Being self-reliant empowers you to cut costs as you control your Web presence.

A potential drawback to a turnkey solution can be utility (what it can or can't do). If your business Website requires extensive interaction with other Websites, or if it needs to dovetail into other applications on your computer or the Internet (like your accounting or inventory programs), a turnkey site may not be the best choice. Some turnkey packages can communicate with your existing office programs, while others cannot. The utility of a particular turnkey solution depends on the total package that a company provides, and you must compare options to determine what best fits your needs.

There is a growing variety of turnkey solutions available. Many companies offer package deals with increasing prices dependent upon features and benefits. A few companies offer complete solutions at one flat-rate price, rather than cutting out functionality based on the price tag.

When shopping for a turnkey solution, find one that provides periodic updates as Internet technology improves. Do not settle on one that stagnates in the face of newer technology. Support and upgrades are important, so take the time to research your available options. Are upgrades to your Website free, or does it cost money to buy a newer version? If a new feature or tool is developed by the turnkey solution provider, does it become part of your package, or is it only available to new customers? Most importantly, is there someone you can call if you need help, or is the company completely hands-off with supporting your needs?

Turnkey packages represent huge strides forward in Website development, and the turnkey market is becoming more competitive as new ideas are introduced through this forward-thinking technology.

One of the best turnkey solutions I have found is from a company called *Market America, Inc*, which offers complete turnkey packages along with the help of free, live technical support at a reasonable, flat-rate monthly hosting fee. In addition, the *Market America* solution also provides a *Design Center* offering many traditional developer services along with their solid (and continually advancing) turnkey package capabilities.

Due to the significant capabilities, simplicity, and affordability of recent Website technology, turnkey solutions are gradually replacing many Websites previously provided by traditional developers and do-it-yourself programs.

Turnkey solutions offer a feature-rich balance between usefulness and professional appearance at both a significant cost and time savings. If you shop for a package in the turnkey market, make an "apples to apples" comparison between providers to ensure that you are getting both the capability *and* the support that you need for an effective online package.

Advantages and disadvantages of a Turnkey Solution Website:

👍 You control content without needing technical or programming knowledge.

👍 They cost less than traditional solutions, and the sites are often value-packed with tools, controls, and services.

👍 Your site *usually* has a professional look.

👎 Some turnkey programs are limited in content management control and may produce sites with a simple, amateur, or template-like look.

👎 You may be confined to host with the provider.

☺ Shop around before you buy to compare the features and benefits of different packages.

About Website Hosting

Storage Space

Website hosting, simply speaking, means rented storage space on the Internet. The storage space is for your Web pages and related files. The amount of space is measured in terms of individual characters (letters and numbers) called *bytes*. Storage space ranges from a few megabytes (millions of bytes) to several gigabytes (billions of bytes). The amount of space you need depends on the types and ranges of services, files, and media you plan to use.

If you plan on having a basic Website that uses pictures and files optimized for the Web (meaning that they have small file sizes), you may initially only need a few megabytes of storage space. Later, you may need significantly more space if you plan on adding large files, sound, video, and extensive amounts of information to your Website.

For the average Website, 100 megabytes of space is ample, and some hosting companies may offer significantly more space to allow for future expansion. Whether a provider offers 300 megabytes or three gigabytes of space, excess space is something that is nice-to-have but not a must-have.

"Up-Time" Reliability

Reliability is a key issue when you own a Website. The hosting service that supports your site should be able to claim a 99.9% up-time to ensure that your site is "never" inaccessible. Ask hosting companies what their specific performance is, how often their systems are down for maintenance, whether their maintenance activity affects the site accessibility, etc.

Hosting server location is the other piece of the reliability puzzle that you need to address. Will your Website be hosted on a computer in someone's garage, or is it maintained in a secure, climate controlled facility?

Answers to these kinds of questions are important to ensure that your online business presence is well-protected and always available to your customers.

Tools and Resources

Your hosting service may include management tools to help you maintain your Website. If you use a do-it-yourself Website solution, the hosting company you choose may include support for third-party add-on Website programs to enhance your site's capability.

A traditional developer may provide hosting services which include all of the space, tools, and resources that your particular situation requires. If they do not provide Website hosting (in other words, they are not a complete solution provider), then you will need to find a hosting service that offers appropriate support elsewhere. The developer should be able to recommend a compatible, reputable hosting company.

For turnkey solutions, the hosting is usually included with the package that you purchase. Tools, reports and support will normally be included as part of the monthly hosting and management fee. The specific tools will vary depending on the package you buy. Decide upon a company that allows flexibility and expansion as your business grows online.

Regardless of which type of Website solution you decide upon, ensure that your tools and resources are included *in addition to* the storage space that is available as part of your hosting service. Otherwise, if your hosting provider adds a-la-carte tools that use a portion of your allowed storage space, be certain that the remaining space available is sufficient to host your site.

Bandwidth and Transfer Limitations

As a Website owner, bandwidth means two things to you: speed and volume of information. Bandwidth translates to how fast information is sent to and from your site and how much is allowed to be transferred on a monthly basis.

When visitors use the Internet, they may be using a slow (dial-up) connection or a high speed (cable, DSL service, etc.) connection. Whichever Internet service they are using, your Website will appear on their screen as quickly as allowed by the bandwidth connection that they have. You can't control their bandwidth, but you do want to ensure that your hosting service can meet or exceed the bandwidth demands that are placed on it from your customers' Internet Service Providers. The connection will probably not be adequate if your site is hosted from someone's garage on a home computer or small network server.

Transfer volume is the amount of information (in megabytes or gigabytes) sent to or from the hosting service provider on a monthly basis. If you use a hosting provider that limits the amount of monthly information allowed to be sent, and if you have large files that your visitors download from your site, then you may quickly exceed the bandwidth limitation of your account before the end of the month.

Find a hosting company that allows sufficient bandwidth, preferably an unlimited amount per month. It will hurt your business if your customers are greeted with the message, "We're sorry, this site has exceeded its monthly bandwidth limit. Please try again later." when they visit your site.

Backups

Ensure that your hosting company does periodic backups to protect your site and data. If you created the Website yourself, then you should also retain a copy of the site on your own computer. If you use a turnkey solution in which you update your own site, ensure that your service provider keeps your site backed up on an ongoing basis.

Finding a good hosting provider:

☺   Find a hosting service that provides more space and bandwidth than you need so you can grow.

☺   Look for value-added hosting providers that offer free services, tools, reports, etc.

☺   Ensure your hosting service has free, accessible tech support.

Section Three: Questions & Answers

Topics Covered:

What You Should Ask

Pricing and Costs

Site Design and Features

and

Website Services

Q & A

An Unhealthy Web Developer – Client Relationship

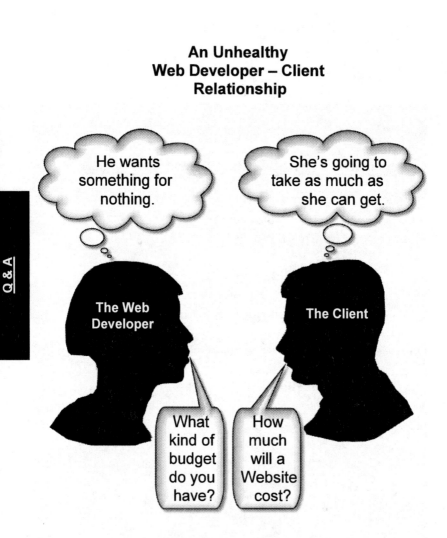

The best way to avoid starting off on the wrong foot with suspicion and distrust is to be an informed consumer who knows what to expect from your Website solution provider.

What You Should Ask

If you have ever shopped for a computer, then you know how easy it is to be "sold" on the next best upgrade. For just a few dollars more, you can double your hard drive's capacity. Then, for just a few extra dollars, you can add twice the memory. As long as you're doing that, it only takes a few more dollars to get the faster processor. Sooner or later, the $10 here, $40 there, all add up to several hundreds of dollars built into the price tag. Of course, it costs less to buy it up front as part of a package than to upgrade piecemeal later. So you walk out of the store wondering, "How did I spend $2000 on a computer when I planned to spend $1200?" Welcome to the world of upselling.

The same thing can happen to you with your Website solution if you're not careful. In terms of economies of scale, Internet solution providers often package features together at one discounted price tag. You may find that a particular package delivers more than you need but at a cost savings—sort of like buying a value meal that includes a burger, fries, and soda for $6 at a fast food place, rather than buying the burger and drink individually for $6.15. (Even though you didn't want the fries, it's just cheaper to get them packaged with what you do want for less money.)

In many cases, your business will eventually grow into the extra features that are offered as part of an online solution package, so having some bells and whistles along with your Website and hosting package is not a bad thing. There are two specific areas to watch out for in the package deals, however. The first is if the consultant who helps you works on commission based on the sales price. The second is if the Website *hosting* cost increases as features, tools, and services are added. If the solution provider that you work with has incentive to sell you a more robust package, then they may try to convince you to upgrade against your best interests. Be sure you have a clear understanding of what will be included in your solution before you agree to buy, and be wary of sales people who upsell you into paying for more features without first learning about your needs.

Paying more than you should and being sold more than you need are examples of being *oversold*. Be careful not to pay high monthly fees for a package that has excessive features that you will not use. Hosting alone is rented storage space on the Web and should be reasonably inexpensive. Services may add a modest amount to the monthly costs, but you should not get gouged multiple times for the same features.

For example, if your monthly Website hosting costs $20 or $30, but adding e-commerce capability to the site (just the shopping cart and catalog, not including a merchant account) adds $1200 to the cost of the site *plus* an additional $100 per month for hosting, then you need to ask "why?"

Once you have paid a developer to program a shopping cart into your site, should you really continue to pay monthly for it to be there? The server space that a shopping cart and catalog use is likely within the amount that would come with your hosting package anyway, regardless of adding the shopping cart and catalog. Are you being charged extra for additional space you won't use? Why pad the pockets of a hosting service provider by paying extra for it monthly?

On the other hand, some solution providers include e-commerce capability with the monthly hosting service (non-transferable) rather than charging you to program it into your Website's design. In such instances, you are not paying for the capability twice, but need to consider that your hosting options may be confined to doing business with that provider in order to use the shopping cart and catalog.

We have discussed upselling and being *oversold*, but we also need to address the other extreme: the bare-bones Website that is insufficient to meet your needs. If you are too conservative or not thorough enough when you set out to find a Web solution, you might get *undersold*.

Economies of scale work in your favor when you can implement a Web solution that includes features and benefits that will be used later, if not now. Be careful not to spend hundreds now, only to find out that in a year's time you need to spend thousands to have your site reworked to meet your emerging needs. It's much better to get a value package that you will evolve with over time as long as you don't get oversold on services you don't need.

If you are unsure about what you need, confer with a knowledgeable, experienced consultant prior to buying anything. Otherwise your initial Website may meet your needs in the short-term, but when you invest in a solution, you should be thinking two to three years down the road. Give yourself and your business room to grow online. A qualified Web consultant will ask you questions that align your Website solution with your company's strategic plan and help you find a balanced, expandable solution to meet your needs. If you have developed a good rapport with your Web consultant and the advice they give makes sense for your business's short and long-term plans, it's probably best to go with it. They get paid to guide you in the right direction.

If the idea of approaching a Web developer still intimidates you, there are several leading questions you can ask that will help you collect information to make a solid decision. Asking the right questions will lead you to the right package. The package you decide upon should cover the three essential elements of The Website Triangle and include a hosting package that helps you effectively manage your Web presence.

The remaining parts of this Q&A section include questions that are categorized by topic. You may not find every question applicable, so consider your unique requirements and choose the questions that best fit your situation. Each question is fairly straightforward, but unfortunately answers in the Web development industry aren't always so simple. Consequently, it is important to have a little more background when asking the questions.

The answers that follow not only address the "what" but also provide the "why" generally related to each question. The solution provider you decide upon should be able to satisfy your questions in enough detail to earn your confidence. These answers are useful for do-it-yourself and turnkey solutions, too.

Questions to Ask as you Shop

Pricing and Costs

Q: How much will the Website cost?
A: If you work with a traditional developer, anticipate that you will receive an itemized breakdown of a-la-carte features and benefits in response to this question. They should require a consultation before answering the question. If you are given a price quote without any questions about your company's or organization's requirements, my recommendation is to steer clear. It is not reasonable to be quoted a set price, arbitrarily, unless you are evaluating a turnkey package which is more likely to be priced at a flat rate.

When you ask the price question, expect a series of questions to be asked of you in return. When the solution provider responds in-kind by asking questions, it is probably not an attempt to "flip" the conversation on you; rather, it's a legitimate attempt to serve your needs and quantify the price realistically. Web developers do not stay in business long if they earn a reputation for constantly delivering a product over budget, so it's in their best interests as well as yours to be as accurate as possible from the onset. Give detailed answers so you receive a solid, reliable price quote.

Additionally, if the solution provider offers both traditional and turnkey options, the questions they ask will help them narrow down your needs so they can recommend the best fit for you.

Later in this section we will cover average costs for various features and services that make up your site.

Q: What is the payment schedule for the Website?
A: Most developers will want some earnest money up front, called a *developer's fee*. In the case of a traditional developer, the developer's fee is paid in advance of any work being performed. It is typically enough to offset any overhead costs to the solution provider (for example, to pay their programmers' wages) if you opt *not* to purchase the Website from them once you see an initial conceptual design. In the case of a turnkey solution, a development fee is usually a down payment on the flat rate of the Website package to cover licensing and setup.

Once you have paid the developer's fee, the balance of payments is commonly made in phases. Each phase represents a checkpoint in the site's development. Traditional developers use these checkpoints to verify that they are progressively working to your satisfaction as they bill you incrementally for design work. The amount will generally be some pre-defined portion of the overall quote plus any hourly or incidental fees incurred as a result of changes and rework. A turnkey solution payment plan will often bill in monthly intervals, spreading the flat rate balance over a given number of months at some interest rate.

If you are shopping for a traditional developer, find one that agrees to apply the development fee to the overall cost of the site (assuming you buy a solution from them), rather than itemizing it separately on the invoice as a non-refundable cost above and beyond the site design. In many cases reputable developers charge the fee to protect themselves against "tire kickers," rather than as a means of adding extra profit to their bottom line. Otherwise, developers would be vulnerable to paying programmers to create ideas for curious but non-serious inquiries that waste their time.

If you are shopping for a turnkey solution, the developer's fee is usually referred to as a *setup fee* or *activation fee*. Consider service providers that allow you to review and evaluate their solutions free of charge (on a free trial basis) before you have to put any money towards such fees. It's better to find a company that straightforwardly lets you "try before you buy," rather than one that requires you to pay up front with the promise of a full or partial refund if you change your mind. The best turnkey solution providers will offer a completely risk-free satisfaction guarantee in which you can try out the solution first and still offer some kind of money-back provision if you are dissatisfied with their service after activating the site.

Q: How much is the hosting, and what services or features are included with it?
A: Hosting, itself, should be a relatively minimal cost to your Website solution. On the average, you can expect to pay somewhere between $5 and $20 per month for basic hosting if you use a do-it-yourself Website. The hosting does not include pricing to outsource the different facets of your Internet solution.

Recall that simple hosting is nothing more than renting space on the Internet. For an effective Website solution, your site will need to be more than simply "shelved" on the World Wide Web. Managing your Website will incur some additional costs that can be provided individually or priced as part of a package deal.

For example, through a traditional developer, Search Engine Optimization (SEO) may cost anywhere between $300 to $1200 per month or more, depending on the level of service that you require. For that kind of money, you should anticipate that the solution provider will perform all of the optimization work on your behalf, and report the actions and results to you on a monthly basis. They may offer the service at a discount in conjunction with hosting.

Website metrics reporting is another important service instrumental to your Website's success. Metrics analysis and reporting is intertwined with the SEO and search engine submission process. Metrics provide the tools to manage the marketing, promotion, and submission for your Website. Traditional solution providers will usually offer this service a-la-carte for an additional fee but may alternatively include some user-friendly tools with a hosting package for a few extra dollars per month.

In other words, if you pay the developer separately to analyze and compile Website usage statistics for your site, you might spend between $75 and $150 per month, whereas a hosting package that *includes* automated reporting services might be in the neighborhood of $50 to $75 monthly.

Turnkey solutions may also offer package pricing for hosting and management tools. For a basic hosting package that includes SEO, metrics, and other tools packaged along with the rented Web space, the range of services can reasonably cost between $30 and $100 per month. Some turnkey providers divide their hosting packages into basic and premium categories, adding more bells and whistles to the package as they increase storage capacity and bandwidth limits with higher monthly prices. In such cases, it can be very easy to get oversold on a solution. Perform a solid *needs assessment* (described later in the Decision Process section of this book) prior to choosing a hosting service provider.

To illustrate the point, let's assume that your Website requires hosting space of 30 megabytes, and you also need a secure shopping cart (e-commerce functionality) for your business. You might find a turnkey solution provider that offers 100 megabytes of space online for $35 per month without e-commerce, but to get the shopping cart, they require you to upgrade your hosting service to a $125 per month package that includes one gigabyte of hosting space and other features that are in excess of your needs.

The upsell of extra bells and whistles to justify higher monthly package prices is usually something you can avoid. Look for a solid, expandable solution at a flat rate price. $35 to $70 is a reasonable monthly fee for a capable turnkey solution that includes hosting, e-commerce, search engine submission tools, and analysis tools. Compare the value between packages.

Q: How much will it cost to make changes or updates to my Website on an ongoing basis?
A: If you have ever purchased a printer for your computer, then you know that printer manufacturers aren't just in the business of selling hardware; they're in the business of selling ink. It may have been a surprise to you (the first time you had to replace all four colors in your ink jet printer) to learn that new ink can cost more than the printer itself. *"Wow, what a racket!"* you may have thought. Printer manufacturers

seem to pack an array of features into versatile, multi-function devices and almost give them away at disposable prices, knowing that you'll be back again and again to replace the consumable ink or toner.

What they didn't collect up front, they collect over the lifetime value of you, their loyal customer. Think of your initial Website design and the subsequent, ongoing updates to your site as a loose parallel to the printer scenario.

When you approach a Website developer to put a site design together for you, one of the most important details you can learn about will be the ongoing costs of maintaining the site. Monthly changes can quickly become a *cash cow* to a Website designer since ongoing updates to your Website's content can be time consuming yet essential to an effective solution.

Changes are foreseeable to varying degrees based on the type of business you own. Real estate agents, for example, have a constant influx of new listings and need to update current listings with status, price, and other details. Flower shops must update their arrangements and bouquets monthly to reflect various holidays: Valentine's Day, Mother's Day, Father's Day, Easter, etc. Clothing stores, cosmetics retailers, and other seasonally influenced businesses must rotate their content to reflect the latest colors, styles, and so forth.

Hourly changes add up quickly depending on the level of detail on your site. For a simple, animated seasonal banner ad, it may only take the better part of an hour to create, edit, and post to your site. In contrast, adding multiple pages or hundreds of catalog items to your site may take several days.

There is nothing more impressive than a finely choreographed multimedia site, complete with interactive features and forms. The downside is that projects somehow seem to come together so *slowly* when you are being billed on an *hourly* basis. Interview your solution provider thoroughly to ensure they are able to meet your ongoing needs—and that you won't be paying hourly for their learning curve if they lack experience where you need it.

Updating content is essential to the effectiveness of your Web presence because some search engines evaluate the freshness of your content as part of their ranking criteria. Stale content may translate to falling placement on various search engines. Knowing this, a conscientious solution provider will recommend that you at least make some simple changes to your site on a periodic basis to help maintain or elevate your Website's positioning in search engine rankings. Additionally, customers get bored seeing the same old material on your site. Updates keep your site interesting.

Too often, addressing the maintenance costs of a Website is an afterthought for a non-Web savvy business owner. If you have never managed a Website before, your Web developer may know better than you do how often you will need to make changes. They *may* not address the potential concerns or objections relevant to Website maintenance when you initially agree to buy a site from them. If you weren't considering the ongoing costs of updating your Website, this particular unforeseen expense can later be a rude awakening.

Expect fees for Website work from a traditional developer to range between $80 and $100 per hour, realizing that the actual rate will vary from city to city based on the local economy. Developers will often prorate their fees into fifteen minute or half-hour increments to accommodate more reasonable billing for smaller jobs. Understanding that fresh content is important to your continued online success, some developers may offer a pre-determined number of updates per month to make simple changes to your site's text or pictures. For more substantial changes, a-la-carte pricing may apply to graphics work, additional pages, adding items to a catalog, and so forth *with or without* hourly fees.

Read the fine print. Although basic content changes to a Website may take only a few moments to perform, you will sometimes find that development companies tack on the words "or any part thereof" to their hourly rates. Shop around for developers who will honor a prorated rate so you don't pay an hour's worth of money for a five minute job.

As with any type of time-based billing, the amount of time it takes for your job to be completed will largely depend on the skill level and experience of the individual doing the work. To standardize rates for particular tasks, some companies have turned to a fee structure that bills a specific rate for certain work, much like the automotive service industry has done for years. In car repair, you may need your alternator replaced and the shop charges you a set fee based on the amount of labor hours published in a service manual, regardless of how long the job actually takes.

Drawing the parallel to the Web development industry, you may be billed a flat fee to add a page to your site, whether it takes 20 minutes or two hours to complete. Billing in this way ensures that the development company makes a consistent amount of money per job, while also ensuring that you are not unfairly charged an excess amount for a slow worker. Shop around to be sure that you know the best pricing and billing practices between solution providers in your area. Based on your particular business, if you anticipate that you will need frequent or substantial updates to your site, this cost consideration can weigh heavily on your final choice of a provider.

The practice of paying a developer to make changes to your Website most commonly relates to traditional solution providers, not turnkey solutions. After all, one of the hallmark features of turnkey solutions is that they provide content management tools that allow you to maintain the site yourself, rather than pay someone to do it. There are some exceptions, however, as many traditional developers have begun adding content controls to their projects.

Obtain quotes for your project both with and without content management tools to see if there is an appreciable difference in project costs. Some designers charge higher prices to include content management tools. There are three reasons for the price increase. First, it takes time to program the tools into the site. Second, the tools add significant value to your site. Finally, the developer potentially loses income from empowering you to update the site yourself, so a higher price on the front end of such a project offsets some of their long-term losses.

In comparison, turnkey solutions usually include content management tools to allow you to make your own changes at no additional cost, although some turnkey providers assess a per-change fee once the initial site design is set up. Shop around to find a provider that offers technical support assistance for customers who make their own changes, adding yet another layer of support to your Website solution. Some of the better turnkey service providers offer traditional design services along with the content management tools, empowering you to make basic monthly changes yourself while providing an hourly or a-la-carte fee structure to complement your own efforts.

Costs vary with turnkey solutions, but "*free*" is always a good description to look for when it comes to technical support. It is reasonable to expect to pay something if you use a design service to make the changes for you, but with a turnkey provider, such services should realistically be at or even slightly below the going rates for those of a traditional developer. The hybrid of using a turnkey package that also offers development services gives you the best of both worlds between turnkey and traditional solution providers.

Q: What do additional pages cost if I need to expand my site later?
A: Although this question may appear redundant with the previous question about ongoing updates and changes to your Website, there is a big difference between changing "*happy*" to "*glad*" in the text of a paragraph on a page and adding an entirely new

page to your Website (which involves updating the menus, navigation bars, and links on other pages to accommodate the new addition). Obviously, adding a new page involves more work.

Expanding upon the answer to the previous question, there can be a significant difference in costs between a turnkey solution and a traditional developer for adding pages. A traditional developer will usually charge $80 to $100 per page added. The price may include a pre-determined number of text and image elements, perhaps two paragraphs and two pictures, for example. For anything beyond the standard fare, you can expect to pay a-la-carte fees and hourly rates for the work to be done on the page.

Turnkey packages work a bit differently. Some offer additional pages for no charge at all, while others offer a specified number of pages included with your Website, and additional pages may or may not be added for a fee.

Beware of turnkey providers that base monthly hosting fees on a particular number of pages. A $35 to $50 per month hosting from such a company may include up to five pages, but when you add a sixth page, you could unwittingly "wander into the deep end of the swimming pool" at $70 (or more) per month for the automatic switchover to their next higher hosting package. This type of fee structure is more common among turnkey solutions that advertise *free* Websites with no setup or activation fees, just hosting.

If you use a turnkey solution rather than a traditional developer, find a company that offers unlimited free additional pages with no change to the monthly hosting fee. Many features of turnkey packages are proprietary to the hosting service, so plan ahead for future expansion of your Website. You don't want the possibility of experiencing a dramatic increase in monthly costs if you later cross a page limit threshold discussed in the fine print. It can be frustrating, time consuming, and expensive if you decide to move your Website to another company's hosting because of such an oversight.

Q: How much does it cost for a-la-carte features, such as maps, forms, Flash, a shopping cart, etc?
A: This is a difficult question to answer because no standard rate applies from one developer to the next. Citing national averages would have little relevance since service provider prices differ significantly with the cost of living from city to city. The local economies in Seattle, WA, and Minneapolis, MN, for instance, have significantly higher costs of living than those in Indianapolis, IN, and Topeka, KS. Their average prices differ accordingly. Therefore, averaging the costs nationally provides a ballpark figure but results in a skewed figure from a *local* service provider standpoint.

There are two general schools of thought regarding traditional Website developers. This is where we can usually see a distinction between Website developers and Website solution providers as defined earlier on page 68. The Website developer typically has a price-per-feature fee structure that can be applied to a given list of itemized functionality that you request, whereas a Website solutions provider tends to operate more on a consultation basis, pricing your Website individually based on a combination of features and services. As with anything else, there is a middle ground where some companies price solutions based on a combination of cost-per-item and a consultation. The key to not getting oversold is to understand the value of what you want, so you can discern whether the consultation is focused on fair pricing to meet your needs or focused on feeling out what you are able or willing to pay.

To give you a sense of what to expect from Web companies around the United States, I looked on numerous search engines using the keywords "Website Design." I selected a minimum of 10 companies in each of 32 cities to obtain quotes for price comparisons.

I emailed an identical quote request to each of the companies. The email was general enough to leave terms such as "reasonable budget" up to the developers' discretion. Predictably, many companies replied with a series of consultation questions and requests for a discussion prior to arriving at a price. Equally anticipated, some companies provided a-la-carte pricing.

In sending the quote requests, I was particularly careful not to indicate that the quotes would be used in a buyer's guide of any kind. Doing so would have been akin to walking into a restaurant and letting the manager know that I was going to publish a written review of their service. Obviously, in such a case, I would have received extraordinary service which would have skewed results. My request for Website quotes had to be done as a "secret customer" to ensure I received impartial treatment.

I collected the data and averaged the prices within each city. If a particular company provided an unrealistically lowball number for the specifics that I requested (like one I received for $200) or an arbitrary, outlandishly high number (for example, one response came back as a one-liner reply that simply stated "About $30,000.") its individual quote was not included in the average.

Some of the developers suspected that I worked with Websites and confronted me on the topic. If asked, I explained the nature of the quote request—that the numbers were being used to research Web prices around the country for a book. When those companies learned that their numbers were to be used in a buyer's guide, many of them offered to amend their quotes. To prevent skewing the results in reporting average Website costs, their figures were also discarded. The only data used in the computed averages came from companies that submitted price quotes with meaningful, legitimate, untainted cost explanations.

The averages provide you with a benchmark for each particular locality. Keep in mind, they are *generalities* that you can use as a guideline. The pricing for your project may vary significantly based on your unique requirements. Although I can not attest to what the final, actual costs would have been from any of the companies if I had bought a site, the figures collected were generally consistent within each locality.

In all, over 400 companies provided information or pricing data for Website solutions. Each company received exactly the same email request for information. The generic price quote request they received is shown on the following page.

Website Quote Request

To whom it may concern:

I am looking for pricing information to set up a Website. I know that there are a number of factors involved, but assume a reasonable budget set aside for the project.

Please let me know your company's pricing for the following elements in producing a site. **I have made the list in a bullet-fashion so that you can easily hit "Reply" and add the line item costs at the end of each line**, *thereby not taking up too much of your time in drafting a response. I will need this information as soon as possible as I have a self-imposed deadline within the next week or so:*

- *Price for general development, if any:*
- *Price per Page (assume 7 pages, and assume two to three paragraphs per page and 3 to 5 images per page):*
- *Price to add a simple Flash banner of about 8 seconds run-time (whether hourly for design work or per second of run-time):*
- *Price to add a secure e-commerce shopping cart to the site, equipped to sell 50 individual items:*
- *Price to add a form (like a feedback form or questionnaire) to the site:*
- *Price to add an interactive/embedded map with driving directions:*
- *Price for traffic analysis tools/reports:*
- *Price for monthly hosting:*
- *Price to optimize it for the search engines (Initial / Monthly):*
- *Price for technical support on the site if I need help with it:*
- *Price to make changes or updates to the site:*
- *Also, can I have documents (like PDF files or text files) that customers can link to/download? Price to add?*

Thank you very much in advance for your reply. I look forward to hearing back from you.

Regards,
Tom Elliott

The pricing information on the following pages reflects the average costs that were obtained from the service providers in each of the 32 cities. You will find the averages in the table on page 104.

Remember, the cost information in the table does not reflect pricing from any one company. Your own research may yield higher or lower numbers. The data used to arrive at the average costs came from Web developers that were found in top rankings on local searches in the search engines. Therefore the pricing information was found the same way that the average consumer would locate a Website developer.

Although the pricing information is applicable at the printing of this book, prices will obviously change with the market over time. However, there are some consistencies that will remain relevant regardless of the going rate for Websites in a given locality. You can learn a few things about trends in the Website market by breaking down the price tag of a solution into the component parts of design, hosting, SEO, and hourly maintenance costs.

The data from city to city indicates that Websites are "packaged" differently depending on where you buy them. Some companies tend to weight the bulk of their pricing in design, while others seem to put more value on ongoing SEO work. In some cases, the *overall* price to get started with a Website was similar from one city to the next, but considering how the pricing breaks down, you could save money by obtaining different parts of your solution from different cities. In the Internet economy, location of the provider does not matter.

Refer to the table on the next page. The data from the quote requests is arranged in columns on the table as follows:

- **Site Design Costs:** includes setup fees, page development, the shopping cart, map, form, and initial Search Engine Optimization.
- **Monthly Hosting & Tools:** includes hosting, Web analytics tools, traffic reporting, and other routine monthly fees.
- **Monthly SEO costs:** includes a combination of optimization, adjustment, and submission on an ongoing basis.
- **Hourly fees:** includes work done on a one-time or ongoing basis.
- **Average 1st Month Costs:** reflects the anticipated costs to get the initial site up and running, hosted, and optimized in terms of overall project costs.

When you price Websites on your own, the rule of thumb is that site development and price-per-page make up the largest expenses in a Website design. The next two highest costs are a secure e-commerce shopping cart and the optimization of the site, respectively. From the quotes I received, e-commerce and SEO each account for approximately $800 to $1200 in development costs. Depending on the scope of the project, the variance in price among e-commerce and SEO can be several thousand dollars.

Before a developer begins work on your project, it is important to ask the right questions, give a detailed description of the project requirements, and have a thorough consultation to obtain the most accurate price possible. Any project can be subject to unforeseen challenges and potential cost overruns, but good communications help to minimize such obstacles.

Q & A

Benchmarks for Traditional Web Design Solutions

City \ Costs	Site Design Costs	Monthly Hosting & Tools	Monthly SEO Costs	Hourly Fee	Average 1st Month Costs
Atlanta	$4418	$49	$1883	$71	$5879
Baltimore	$3579	$37	$1538	$74	$4634
Boston	$5075	$37	$100	$82	$5128
Chicago	$4837	$34	$1150	$93	$5561
Cleveland	$7640	$50	$50	$89	$7670
Dallas	$6818	$32	$590	$89	$7923
Denver	$5244	$90	$229	$101	$5465
Greensboro	$5969	$43	$370	$69	$6323
Harrisburg	$3088	$78	$35	$75	$3183
Houston	$9460	$257	$317	$102	$9907
Indianapolis	$3930	$35	$263	$83	$4228
Jacksonville	$2795	$47	$200	$63	$2908
Las Vegas	$2701	$20	$79	$63	$2747
Los Angeles	$4275	$56	$466	$96	$4331
Louisville	$5933	$34	$349	$70	$6194
Miami	$6317	$17	$1125	$67	$7078
Minneapolis	$8688	$45	$500	$107	$9233
New York City	$4550	$50	$1000	$98	$4933
New Orleans	$4560	$109	$600	$74	$4789
Newark	$3700	$50	$50	$78	$3750
Norfolk	$7034	$20	$318	$86	$7253
Phoenix	$5450	$66	$368	$60	$5771
Pittsburgh	$2383	$22	$466	$57	$2405
Richmond	$8917	$45	$1625	$110	$7523
Sacramento	$4783	$19	$195	$95	$4899
San Antonio	$6718	$39	$180	$86	$6801
Scottsdale	$3292	$24	$300	$67	$3408
Seattle	$9733	$38	$440	$116	$9990
St. Louis	$10100	$90	$400	$110	$10293
Tampa	$3699	$82	$538	$20	$4139
Topeka	$2345	$25	$466	$62	$2370
Wichita	$2833	$29	$75	$63	$2877
NATIONAL AVERAGE*	**$5339**	**$52**	**$508**	**$81**	**$5593**

*The national averages were smoothed by averaging the averages of each city in the table.

Each city has similarities between Web developers in the way that categories are priced. For example, there is a tendency for companies in some cities to include SEO in the bid for the site with small monthly payments to maintain it, while in others cities, companies do not include SEO in an initial Website development and bill it completely separately.

In other words, there are notable differences in the Website market from city to city. The SEO average prices in Boston and Cleveland seem disproportionately low when compared to those of Baltimore or Atlanta. However, notice that the site design costs are comparatively higher in Boston and Cleveland. This is due to the tendency for Web developers in Boston and Cleveland (from companies that responded to my inquiry) to include initial SEO in the price of the site design while charging less money for monthly Website maintenance and search engine resubmission. Take regional factors such as these into account when you do your own pricing research.

Prior to committing to a developer, do some similar marketing research in your own locality. Technology changes quickly and along with it, the marketplace. The best way to make sure you are getting the lowest price for the best service is to do an apples-to-apples comparison before putting any money into the hands of a service provider. If someone tries to pressure you into a buying decision by warning that their pricing is only applicable during their consultation, and that your site will cost more money if you delay, walk away. Remember, you are investing in an online business solution— not buying into a timeshare sales pitch. Your Website should not be a pressure sale.

Q: Is any search engine optimization (SEO) included in the cost of the site or the monthly hosting?
A: In all likelihood, *ongoing* Search Engine Optimization is not included when you purchase a Website. SEO is a service that you will probably have to pay for on a monthly basis. Some Traditional Web developers do not offer SEO at all, and they will refer you to partnered companies that specialize in SEO.

Turnkey Solutions may include SEO tools with their hosting service. If you use such tools to submit yourself to search engines, become familiar with guidelines for when and how to do so. Submitting too often or submitting sites with problematic content can have negative effects on your search engine placement and be counterproductive to your business. Find a turnkey solution provider whose technical support offers guidance on how to use the tools effectively.

Optimizing a Website and submitting it to search engines are two very different processes. *Optimizing* is preparing your site to be ranked well, whereas *submitting* it is "waving the flag" so that search engines readily look at your site to index it. Even if you use SEO tools to submit your own Website, your site should first be optimized. There is no substitute for a professional SEO firm to optimize your site.

For do-it-yourself Websites, you can manually submit your site to search engines by going to each search engine and looking up the submission policy and process. Of course, you can also find an SEO company or Web solutions provider that provides SEO services and pay for their service independently.

If you dabble with SEO yourself, you can do more harm than good by mishandling your own submission.

Q: Does it cost anything for technical support if I need help with, or have questions about, my Website?
A: With a Traditional Web design there is little need for technical support if the design company also hosts the Website. The Web developers for such companies should ensure that your site functions correctly on the Internet when it is put together.

If you work with a do-it-yourself solution or a design company that does not provide hosting service, tech support to publish the site on the Internet will typically be at hourly rates from the hosting service provider. For technical support related to do-it-yourself programs, software companies provide support resources via phone and the Internet. The support may or may not be free. Some do-it-yourself software companies charge your credit card $25 to $100 per hour for technical support services even if the call is toll-free.

Technical support offered with Turnkey solutions is similar in that it may be free or may incur hourly charges. Be careful. Some turnkey companies advertise the feature that you control your own content, but you may find that they make the changes based on your requests and charge you an hourly fee for the tech support to do so. If you use a turnkey solution, find a company with which you are able to make changes yourself and that provides free technical support to assist you with those changes.

Q&A

Site Design and Features

Q: What should I include (how many pages and what features and benefits) with my initial Website design?
A: The short answer to this question should be, "It depends on your specific needs." At a minimum, however, it is important that your Website includes at least five pages for search engine purposes. More is usually better as long as the content is relevant to your audience and your topic.

Search engines may omit Websites that are fewer than five pages as they lack significant content for keyword relevance. In other words, if you just build a simple, informational Web page versus a Website with several pages for your business, the search engines may not take you seriously. A good developer will answer this question with a thorough consultation to define the requirements for your unique business.

Features for your Website Visitors:

Maps

If you have a physical office or storefront location, consider using a map to your street address. There are several types of maps that you can use on a Website. You could choose a plain, static map that shows your location, or you may opt for an interactive map that allows visitors to zoom in and zoom out, get driving directions, etc. Interactive maps may be free if you do not mind having them appear with third-party advertisements (also called *adware*) displayed from companies that pay to be promoted with the map.

Non-adware versions are also available from various providers, usually for a subscription fee.

Your map can be *embedded* into your Website to make it appear as part of a Web page, or it can be displayed as a pop-up in its own window. Due to the annoyances of adware and pop-ups, an embedded, non-adware version (with or without driving directions) is the best choice from a usability standpoint.

Forms

Forms can be an important addition to your Website. They allow your visitors to interact with your business and provide useful information for customer service. A feedback form (or suggestion box form) should be something you include to collect opinions and requests from your Website's visitors. Other examples of forms include job and account applications, insurance and contractor quotes, tax preparation and estate planning worksheets, dining reservations, salon appointments, medical appointments, and so forth.

Language Translators

If your products and services are sold internationally, or *interculturally*, then having translated versions of your Website is important. By bridging language barriers, you can expand your business into neighborhoods and countries that would otherwise not be inclined or able to do business with you.

Language translation services can be very expensive, and the price will differ significantly between a literal (word for word) and an idiomatic (what is meant in context) translation, so you will need to decide whether it is financially worthwhile to integrate such an option. Some turnkey solution packages and traditional developers can include tools that provide literal multi-lingual versions of your Website at a reasonable cost, which may be a more feasible option (budget-wise) than hiring a translator to convert each page individually.

Databases

Simply stated, a database is a collection of information that can be sorted and displayed in useful ways. Does your Website need a database? If you work with information that your customers, employees, or vendors would want to access and prioritize, then inquire about including databases with your Web design.

Databases can be useful for parts and supply stores, financial establishments, realtors, and more. They offer your customers the ability to sort products or services by category, manufacturer, price, feature, color, or any other characteristic, and display only the ones of interest.

Blogs, Message Boards, and Chat Rooms

People can interact with your business and with other people via Web Logs (Blogs), message boards (forums), and chat rooms (instant messaging). *Blogs* are comparable to diaries or journal entries in which people express their opinions, beliefs, and feedback on whatever topic is being discussed. Similarly, *message boards* are divided into multiple topics, and visitors can post questions, answers, advice, hints, etc. *Chat rooms* allow instant communications between visitors and can be used for customer service, technical support, community discussions, and general pen-pal interaction.

Features to Manage Your Business:

To this point in discussing what your Website should include, we've looked at features available to your visitors and customers. Now let's examine management tools that will benefit you as a business owner. There are multiple applications that can be built into your Website's design to help you improve efficiency by doing business online.

Ask your hosting provider about tools that may be included to assist you in managing forms, databases, information security, and other parts of your Web design.

Contact Management Tools

A contact manager allows you to expand your market. As your Website draws visitors over time, you will want to ensure that their contact information (from questions, requests, and orders) is captured and retained in a customer database. Begin communicating with customers and vendors on a recurring basis to remind them of specials, promotions, and new developments that may interest them.

No, this is not *spam*. *Spam* is unsolicited emails to people with whom you have no established relationship. With a contact manager tool, you would be corresponding with people who have opted to receive your emails.

Web Analytics

Tracking tools that measure traffic to your Website are sometimes called *Web Metrics, Web Trends,* or *Web Analytics.* They allow you to monitor the usage of your Website so you can determine 1) the source of your Web traffic, 2) frequency of visits to each page, 3) keywords people used to find you, and 4) peak usage times on your site. In turn, you can adjust and focus your marketing efforts to maximize your return on investment. A well-defined set of Web analytics tools will help you measure, monitor, adjust, and control search engine optimization efforts.

Q: Is e-commerce available/included with the Website design, and is it secure?
A: First, let's define *e-commerce* and distinguish it from an *online merchant account.* E-commerce simply means the ability to transact business online. An example of this would be if your Website presents an order form to a visitor, collects the relevant information for the order, and allows the customer to print out the form to mail it to you with a personal check. The transaction was facilitated online through your Website and therefore involves electronic commerce.

An online merchant account, on the other hand, is a service tool that allows your customers to make payments for transactions over the Internet. Online payment methods may include credit cards, electronic checks (bank drafts), or credit on account. For e-check and credit card payments, many merchant account providers offer the functionality that allows your Website to interact with the banking system. If your business already accepts credit cards, then you may only need to make a simple phone call to have your merchant account provider add the Internet service. Otherwise, you can apply for a separate merchant account to accept online payments for orders and services via your Website.

E-commerce features can range from very simple (as in accepting donations for a church or non-profit organization), to complex (as in being able to assemble your own computer online through a choice of parts that make up a package). Consider the scope of capability that your business or organization requires, and then examine the options available through each Web solution provider. Be sure that your Website's e-commerce functionality can support the number of individual items that you offer now and is expandable to meet your future retailing requirements.

E-commerce usually combines a catalog of some kind with an online shopping cart. The catalog displays options for a customer to purchase, and the shopping cart keeps track of the items that the customer selects. The shopping cart appears as an online form in which the items are listed and totaled for the purchase. Part of the form includes spaces for the customer to fill in their payment method and shipping address. When the customer clicks a *Purchase* or *Submit Order* button on the form, the contents of the form are sent to your business to be processed.

If the Website is equipped with a merchant account, the payment information is sent to the banking system through something called an *online gateway* which is the merchant account provider's connection to transfer money from one bank to another. Transparently to you, the money for the sale is pulled from your customer's account and deposited into your account, minus some nominal transaction fees that the merchant account provider and credit card companies deduct for their services.

Security is very important with any e-commerce capability. Your customers' personal profiles and banking information must be kept confidential to prevent identity theft or other types of fraud from occurring. Anytime such information is collected and sent over the Internet, it's vital that the information gets scrambled or *encrypted* to ensure that it does not inadvertently end up in the wrong hands.

The level of security is determined by how complicated it is to scramble and unscramble the information being sent. Without getting too technical, it suffices to say that the "buzz words" you want to see when you are shopping for a secure e-commerce solution are "128-bit encryption" or "256-bit encryption."

The details of how each type of scrambling works are not important to running your business. The important point to remember is that you do not want something *less*. The standard for security for the past several years has been 128-bit encryption, used by the banking system to transmit and receive financial data. Financial and government networks are slowly moving to 256-bit encryption which is even more secure. Be sure your e-commerce is equipped with either method.

Doing so adds to the price tag of the site, but it will maintain the confidentiality of your customers' information. If customers' information becomes compromised due to negligence on your part (i.e., not using a secure shopping cart) you may be found liable for any resulting fraud problems or identity theft.

Q: Will the e-commerce services allow me to track orders and inventory as well as provide my customers with order status updates?
A: The extent to which your e-commerce is also a management tool will depend on the programming skill, capabilities, experience, and scope of service that your Website developer provides. Some e-commerce packages allow you to work in conjunction with third party software (inventory and accounting packages) while others are more of a stand-alone product.

Before you read or ask about all of the options available from a particular package, think about the level of service that you need. If you have considered your requirements before you shop for a solution, you will be less likely to be overwhelmed by sales pitches and persuasive marketing literature.

When you evaluate and finally decide upon the scope of your e-commerce package, think about how various tools on a Website might help you track and manage your customers' activities. Ensure that your hosting and management package includes contact management tools to update your customers on order status such as backorders and shipment tracking.

Q: Will I be able to make changes to the site myself, or do I have to pay for a developer to make changes?
A: If you go the traditional developer route, you will likely rely on their professional services to make changes for you. Some developers include content management tools to make basic changes to your

site, but keep in mind that most Website designers make money doing updates, so they may not offer this capability, limit its usefulness, or increase the project costs to include the tools. On the other hand, if you are not inclined to do work on your site yourself, this won't be an issue.

Using a traditional provider, changes normally cost between $80 and $100 per hour, and some developers prorate their hourly rates into 15 or 30 minute intervals. If you pay rates toward the upper end of the price spectrum, ensure that the person you hire is competent and qualified to earn that kind of money, rather than a dabbler who simply uses a do-it-yourself program to create and modify your Website on the premise of being a professional Web designer.

Always get references and look at a portfolio of sample sites. By doing so, even if you have different tastes in the styles that you like or dislike, you will still get insight to the quality of work you can expect.

If you are considering a turnkey solution, there are a few things you must know before deciding upon a provider. Many turnkey providers advertise that you have control over your own content. However, some of them offer this control with limitations. For example, some companies restrict the number of times you are allowed to modify content on a monthly basis.

If you see verbiage that specifies a number of megabytes or gigabytes per month that you can submit, beware. It may not be a factor for your business if you have minimal needs or a basic, informational Website that rarely changes. Website owners that require frequent changes, real estate agents or photographers for example, will find such limits frustrating and costly if the pictures and text updates exceed monthly limits.

Another consideration with turnkey content management solutions is how the changes are actually made. Do you have the ability to make the changes yourself with content management tools? Some companies specify that you must submit a form describing your changes and attach files containing your new content so the turnkey provider that hosts your Website can make the changes for you. Their making the changes might seem appealing at first, but when timing is important, you may find it frustrating to have to wait for the company to get around to it.

The best option for managing your own content through a turnkey solution is to find a package that gives you complete control over content on the site but that offers technical support to assist you in making changes if necessary.

Q: Does the Website include Flash programming?
A: Websites are getting more complex and feature-packed over time. Multimedia (sound, video, animation, and interactivity) is becoming the norm as Web technology advances. Flash, explained simply, is the combination of text, pictures, audio, and video that can add animation to your Website to make your site more exciting, interesting, and interactive.

Although Flash animation has its appeal in finessing a Website, it also has some drawbacks related to links and text properties. For one, it is sometimes difficult to optimize Flash for search engines, potentially affecting Flash-based sites in the search engine rankings.

In layman's terms, words displayed in a Flash animation aren't always text; they're *pictures* of text. Search engines often can not "read" them and compare them to the keywords used in a search by a Web browser. In such cases, there is no connection or relevance to the search. Consequently, Flash-based sites are less likely to be found through natural rankings if relying solely on links or keyword relevance.

Many third-party programs can generate Flash animations. Some of them have compatibility issues with older Web browser versions, and large Flash files can be extremely slow to load over dial-up connections.

Balancing the pluses and minuses to come up with a good solution, you can include a modest amount of Flash animation within the pages of your Website and achieve a positive effect but should consider avoiding a Flash opening page or a completely Flash-based site.

It's interesting to watch the animation and special effects once or twice, but after the novelty wears off, the average consumer wants to find what they're looking for quickly without enduring a video each time they visit your site.

Q: Can the Website include a portfolio of my jobs, before and after pictures, etc?
A: You have probably heard the expression that "a picture is worth a thousand words." Depending on your type of business or organization, one of the most powerful uses of your Website can be showing samples of your work. People trust their eyes and ears more than they rely on conceptual, written descriptions. If you have sample representations of photographic work, before and after pictures of

landscaping jobs, or whatever other examples you can share, your Website will make a dramatic impression on your customers.

Combining stimulating visual and/or audio files with Flash and other enhancing computer programming makes your visitors' experience even more powerful and effective. Don't overdo it though. Animation and sound for the sake of movement and noise can be confusing. Be certain that every bell and whistle you use on your Website is done with a purpose. Otherwise the result will be a cluttered, busy site that looks unprofessional.

Q: For a do-it-yourself or turnkey solution, is the site design restricted to a particular amount of pages or content?
A: Most *do-it-yourself* retail packages have no restrictions on the actual number of pages that you build into the site. There may, however, be limits on the amount of storage space or bandwidth transfers allowed by your hosting provider.

Turnkey solutions vary in the scope of pages that they allow. Find one that allows your site to expand along with your needs. Your Website will be an ongoing project, constantly being updated and enhanced to keep up with the changes in your business. Many turnkey solutions offer an unlimited number of pages within the space provided by their hosting service.

Avoid turnkey packages that only allow five to ten pages, lacking the ability to add any more to the site (or with extra costs for additional pages). Some turnkey providers offer seemingly unbeatable deals (even with free hosting) for a five to ten page Website.

119

In most cases, such providers know that your needs may quickly exceed the capabilities of the free site and that you will require additional features or functionality that incur premium pricing.

Do you think five pages are more than enough? You might be surprised. Perhaps you sell one product and just want a basic site with a Home Page, About Us Page, Place Order Page, Contact Us Page, and Feedback Page. Let's look at what a typical, simple Website that sells a single product might involve:

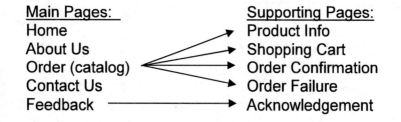

Main Pages: Supporting Pages:
Home   Product Info
About Us   Shopping Cart
Order (catalog)   Order Confirmation
Contact Us   Order Failure
Feedback   Acknowledgement

If you overlooked the Supporting Pages in your estimation, don't feel bad. Most people don't realize that they are individual pages, separate and distinct from the main pages of a Website. The five page site you planned on would actually be 10 pages.

If you have a service-oriented business, you might replace the shopping cart and confirmation pages in the above example with portfolio and testimonial pages. As you can see, even a 10-page limit would not leave you any room to grow. Now consider adding a Frequently Asked Questions (FAQ) Page, additional product or service pages, forms, and document pages. Your site could easily exceed 15 pages without even trying.

For turnkey solutions that offer an unlimited number of pages, the limiting factor on the number of pages your site can have will be the amount of server space your hosting solution provides. A basic Website with a moderate catalog of 200 to 500 items, dozens of pictures, and less than 100 pages will likely be less than 50 megabytes. More elaborate solutions that include video, audio, databases, and file storage may require as much as 200 to 300 megabytes for the same number of pages. A small to medium-size business will typically need fewer than 20 pages for a basic, informational Website.

To give you an appreciation of size and space utilization for Website pages, let's consider an actual example. I once provided a Web solution to a Chamber of Commerce. The site included over 185 pages of text and images, as well as a directory of local businesses. In all, the entire Website required approximately 17 megabytes. Keeping your requirements in perspective, do not get oversold into paying for an excessive amount of unnecessary server space for your Website solution.

While we are on the topic of *site* size, let's briefly discuss *picture* file size. If you take many pictures with a digital camera or scan photos into your computer with a graphics program, the file size of each image makes a big difference when adding pictures to a Website. Pictures that are taken in high resolution for making prints are not good candidates for your Website in their original form. The picture resolution (dimensions as well as dots per inch) must be reduced for the Website.

For example, a 4x6 print may look great on paper at a resolution of 1200 dots per inch, but it will have a file size of several megabytes (millions of small pieces of information). Such a picture will take several minutes to load onto a Web page viewed by a dial-up visitor. The result is that it uses too much server space as well as inconveniences your customers.

By changing the picture to a smaller size at 72 dots per inch and adjusting other features of the picture to prepare it for the Web, your picture will fit better on the screen and still look great but only use a few kilobytes (thousands of small pieces of information) of storage space.

The process of shrinking the file size and adjusting the picture's resolution for your Website is called *optimizing* it for the Web (not to be confused with optimizing a Website for search engines). Pictures load faster and take up less space once they are optimized. Be sure your Website solution provider is familiar with optimizing images for the Internet. If you are doing it yourself, consider picture file size when you upload images to your site.

Q: For a do-it-yourself or turnkey solution, am I confined to working with templates, or is there room for creative design?
A: *Do-it-yourself* programs allow you a fair amount of flexibility. The pre-packaged layouts (templates) that they provide are built to have matching components, navigation bars, and more, but you tend to end up with a home-made looking site if you carelessly cut and paste text and images onto the pages.

If you are comfortable editing your own site, you can depart from the "cookie cutter" look and make your own design by creating unique backgrounds, buttons, borders, banners, etc. By devoting some quality time to your project, you can build an exceptional, professional looking Website with the tools included in the more advanced do-it-yourself programs.

The creative license you have with *turnkey solutions* depends on the individual service provider. Some turnkey solution providers only support a pre-defined selection of Website layouts, and there is little to no room for creativity. In those types of services, the content management tools may allow you to edit the text on the site or change pictures using a library selection of stock photos, but you may not be able to adjust the layout of the site or move paragraphs and images around on a page.

If you use a turnkey provider that has such limited capabilities, you might be able to upload your own pictures or change from one template to another, but in the end your edited version will not look much different from the original layout. Avoid turnkey solutions that confine you to such narrow options.

The best turnkey solutions are those that provide you with a solid starting point populated with suggested text and pictures but allow you to have complete control over content to the extent that you can delete everything down to a blank screen and rebuild the site from the ground up. This level of control essentially gives you the do-it-yourself capability but with tools and services built into the fabric of the Website so you can create a unique, professional design without paying a developer to do the work.

Services

Q: How long will it take to update my Website (basic or major changes to text and images)?
A: If you use a do-it-yourself solution or turnkey solution in which you have real-time control over content updates, you can make and publish simple changes to your Website in a matter of minutes.

If you use a turnkey solution that requires you to submit your changes to a tech support staff to update your site, it may take several hours or days.

Traditional developers typically use a more time consuming proposal, review, and approval process. After you propose changes to your Website content, the Web developer produces a mockup for your review. After you accept the mockup changes, your developer publishes them to the site. The process for making simple changes may be less formalized. However, Web designers usually use some kind of approval process to avoid misinterpreting what you want and to minimize rework.

Q: Are there turnkey solutions that give me complete control but that *also* have design services available to make changes for me?
A: Yes, but they are not very common. Turnkey solution providers tend to be very "hands-off" from getting involved with your Website's design due to staffing reasons. This means that they provide the Web-based software to create your site but are mostly uninvolved in the creation, editing, and maintenance of it.

Some of the better turnkey platforms provide technical support to help you on an as-needed basis. This is a preferable alternative to a hands-off turnkey provider since you can do the basic work on the site yourself but get assistance on performing more complex tasks.

Technical support can be offered in a variety of ways. On the low end, some companies are limited to email support, imposing a time delay in providing the help you need as you have to wait for a reply to your requests. Better turnkey solutions offer live telephone assistance. Some companies even provide remote access and can assume control of your Web browser to either demonstrate how to do the work on your site or do it for you on your own computer screen.

Every turnkey provider is different so research the level of customer service that you can expect from a particular company before you buy your Website. If your computer knowledge and experience set you at ease with learning by trial and error, then you may be fine using a company that expects 100% of your solution to be done by you, with limited guidance via email or through a Frequently Asked Questions (FAQ) page on the company's site.

On the upper end of the spectrum, the best turnkey solution providers also offer the option of traditional developer services to augment your own efforts in updating and maintaining your Website. This gives you the best of both worlds, as you will have the flexibility, control, and cost savings of a turnkey solution combined with the expertise, quality, and options of a traditional Web designer. Refer to page 75 for suggestions.

Q: What tools and services are available to help me optimize and track the usage of my Website and to make sure people can find my site?
A: This question may seem simple, but there is a lot more to it than meets the eye. Website designers specialize in creating the look and feel of your site from the standpoint of what your site's visitors will see. There is much more going on behind the scenes with an *effective* Website solution than what is visible to the public.

A Website that no one can find on the search engines is a liability to your business. You may be the proud owner of a pretty Website, but if it can not be found, the development and hosting costs amount to wasted money. This introduces another cost to your Web solution to make it worthwhile: Search Engine Optimization, commonly called SEO.

SEO is often an add-on sale to your Web solution following the design of your site. Once you've paid your money for the site design, you expect results. If you don't see an influx of phone calls and foot traffic to your business, it may occur to you that people are not finding your new business presence online. In the a-la-carte world of Web solutions, you now must pay more money to have your site optimized and submitted to search engines in order to be found when people search for your business, your products, and your services.

Optimization packages range from paid-for placement to natural ranking adjustment on the Internet. There are several third-party software packages and services to help you promote your Website, and some of the more capable do-it-yourself or turnkey packages include tools so you have an all-in-one approach to your Web solution. Traditional developers should disclose your SEO options in their consultations with you.

Many service providers include tracking tools with their hosting and management packages that report the traffic that your site receives. You should be able to review hits (visits) from individuals, where the traffic originated, keywords that were used to find your site, and many more details.

Q: Am I required to sign a contract for a year (or two, or three, etc.) for hosting services?
A: Much like cellular phone companies or other types of services, many Website development and hosting companies require you to sign a contract. Be sure you understand the commitment terms before you agree to a contract with any Website solution company.

Even if you build your own Website, there will be a hosting agreement for some specified period of time when you use a service provider to put your site on the Internet. Some hosting contracts are month-to-month while others can be for a year or longer. Avoid long term hosting contracts whenever possible. You want to be able to change providers if you outgrow your hosting company's capabilities or experience customer service problems.

Look for a service provider with a satisfaction guarantee. Some offer money back guarantees, while others allow you to cancel your hosting at any time if you are not satisfied with their service.

Avoid the company that attempts to dismiss your concerns about signing their contract, *verbally* assuring you that they will make you happy, "whatever it takes," and that the contract is "just a formality." What is *said* and what is *signed* may not agree, and in the end, service providers seem to remember saying what is written in the contract.

Asking questions and researching your options:

☺ Before you decide which type of solution to get, define your business's specific requirements in writing.

☺ Knowing what to ask about price, design, features, and services makes the task of researching Web solutions easier.

☺ Become familiar with the Website design, hosting, e-commerce and SEO market prices in your local area so you can compare effectively.

☺ Understand how Web developers work and how services are typically rendered so you do not get oversold and so you can manage conversations better with Web developers.

☠ Avoid long-term contracts that bind you into a year or more of doing business with a specific service provider.

☠ Avoid cheap or free sites that limit your expandability or that incur significant fee increases if your requirements change.

Section Four: The Decision Process

Topics Covered:

The Decision Process

and

An Example of the Decision Process

Website Solution Shopping List

Website Design

My Website Budget: $____

Pages I Need:

Home Page
_____
_____
_____
_____
_____
_____
_____
_____
_____

Colors I Like:

1. _____
2. _____
3. _____
4. _____

Features I Need:

- [ ] Secure catalog / shopping cart
- [ ] Map(s) with driving directions
- [ ] Database (able to search / sort)
- [ ] Portfolio display / Job portfolio
- [ ] Flash animation / slide show
- [ ] Video that is playable on site
- [ ] Audio / sound playable on site
- [ ] Event calendar(s) / schedule(s)
- [ ] Forms (job quotes / applications)
- [ ] Translation Tools (multi-lingual)
- [ ] Chat rooms / Instant messages
- [ ] Other: _____

Online Payment Methods I Need:

- [ ] Credit Cards   [ ] E-Checks
- [ ] Other: _____   [ ] None

Search Engine Optimization

My SEO Budget: $____

Keywords I think are important:

_____   _____
_____   _____

My Biggest Competitors:

1. _____
2. _____

Hosting / Management

My Monthly Budget: $____

Domain Name Ideas I Like:

www._____
www._____
www._____
www._____
www._____

Tools I Need:

- [ ] Search Engine Submission Tools
- [ ] Contact Management Tools
- [ ] Content Management / Control
- [ ] Website Metrics / Analytics
- [ ] Other: _____

A shopping list will help you define your needs.

Making a Confident Purchase Decision

The decision to move forward into unfamiliar territory (doing business online) can be intimidating and uncomfortable. It should, though, also be rewarding and profitable. There is no specific right or wrong way to decide how to establish your Web presence, but the key to making a successful transition for your business is to do so *purposefully* and *methodically*.

By now you have enough information to have an idea of what you want. You may, however, feel a bit aimless in how to choose one company or solution type over another. If you are comfortable in your decision making, you can skip this section. But if you need some tips on how to proceed with the Website buying decision, this section proposes a decision making process that will help you.

Description of the Process

When you are prepared to move forward with your decision to invest in a Website solution, start by making a list of services and features that you need on your Website. The list may include maps, translation tools, a catalog and shopping cart, content management tools, etc. It is easier to make your list prior to deciding upon a do-it-yourself program, traditional design, or turnkey package.

Next, for each service you have listed, name as many features, characteristics, and requirements you think you might need. For example, specify the number of items your catalog will carry and what payment methods your shopping cart must accept. For language translation tools, list the specific languages you want to include. Once you have made the detailed list for each service, set the list aside. We will call this your *Needs List.*

From one feature to the next, each provider tries to distinguish themselves from their competition by advertising different combinations of services and functionality. To you, the customer, the result can be a confusing mess of details that is difficult to sort out. Adding to the confusion and frustration, you can become overwhelmed with information if you ask questions of a particular company to clarify what makes it *different* or *better* than another.

Even if you do your due diligence to sort out the details, you may still get stumped when comparing *seemingly identical* packages from one provider to another. When you point out that someone else offers the same basic service for less, you will likely get a response that begins with, "Yes, but ours is better because *blah blah blah...*" followed by a perfectly legitimate explanation (sales pitch) of something that you would be missing if you purchased elsewhere. Back and forth you go. There must be a better way to decide!

The best way to be confident in making your decision is to create a table or chart (a *Solution Provider* chart). Refer to page 135 for an example. List the features and services that you need (from your *Needs List*) down the left column, and then list the potential solution providers across the top. Next, shorten the list of possible providers by eliminating those that do not offer the key functionalities that you require. We'll label the service providers that remain after the cut *"Eligible Service Providers."*

Then create additional charts for each service or feature you need (*Service* charts). Each service chart should contain the specific details, benefits, capabilities, and so forth related to the service. List the details down the left column, and list the *Eligible Service Providers* across the top. The details down the left column should be an all-inclusive combination of features and benefits boasted by the Eligible Service Providers.

If more than one provider offers *exactly* the same service, it is okay to list it on the chart only once. If there are *any differences* in a description, however, make it a unique entry in the chart. Now, for each feature, eliminate the contenders who fail to meet what you wrote on your *Needs List*. The remaining results will help you make an informed decision objectively, rather than get sold on bells and whistles you don't need or won't use.

<u>Example of the Process</u>

To illustrate the decision making process above with a simple example, let's assume that you are inexperienced with Websites, but you know that you need a Website which has the following features:
- A secure shopping cart and catalog
- A map
- Tools to track traffic on your Website
- Language translation functionality

When you create your *Needs List*, be as specific as possible for each of the capabilities that your site must have. For each of the four features in our example, elaborate with specific details that are important. How many items does your catalog need

133

to display? What specific languages do you need to support on your site? When you are finished drafting your Needs List, it may look something like this:

Our Needs List

Secure Shopping Cart and Catalog
-Must support 128-bit encryption
-Catalog must support about 200 items
   (and up to 500 items within six months)
-Accept credit cards
-Accept bank draft / e-checks
-Checkout process allows gift certificates
-Allow customers to buy single items or
   build bundled gift baskets

Map
-Interactive zoom in/zoom out
-Capable of providing driving directions

Tools to Track Traffic on Website
-Show hits on each page of site
-Show source of traffic to site
-Show keywords used to find Website
-Show graphical display / chart of traffic
   pattern over a 30 day period

Language Translation Capability
-Spanish
-French
-English
-Italian
-Allow translations with a single click of
   the mouse

Needs List

Now let's assume that you have found four solution providers who are reputable companies with solid portfolios. The company you decide upon will ultimately include the subjective element of *who you are most comfortable working with*, but it helps to narrow down the options so you can focus on what is most important: which one will best support your business's needs?

The companies depicted in your table can be traditional developers, turnkey solutions, or even do-it-yourself software packages. Our goal is to sort and prioritize our options at this point. In our example, we'll assume the following:

> Company A is a traditional developer.
> Company B is a turnkey solution provider.
> Company C is a retail software package.
> Company D is a turnkey solution provider.

We start with the "big picture" *Solution Provider* chart below to see if any of the four companies simply can't do the job.

		Companies			
		Company A	Company B	Company C	Company D
Features	Shopping Cart	√	√	√	√
	Maps	√	√		√
	Tracking Tools	√	√	√	√
	Translate Tools	√			√

Solution Provider Chart

As you can see, only two of the four companies (companies A and D) offer the necessary features.

135

Therefore, we can reduce the contenders to a more manageable number, and we can evaluate individual charts for the features.

For each feature or service, we create the *Service Charts* that describe the solution provider's specifications down the left column and list the solution providers across the top. As described earlier, the left column should be all-inclusive, so every specification is covered. In our example, we would have separate tables for the shopping cart, map, tracking tools, and translation tools. The analysis for the shopping cart table is shown on the next few pages.

Let's assume that the e-commerce (shopping cart) capabilities for companies A and D are similar but not exactly the same. We need some method to evaluate which one will meet our needs the best, while ruling out extra bells and whistles that should not influence our decision.

From our *Needs List*, we've determined our requirements for a shopping cart to be as follows:
- Must be secure (encrypted) to protect our customers' financial and personal data
- Must be able to accommodate 200 items now and upwards of 500 items later
- Must allow us to accept payments by credit card, e-check, and gift certificates
- Must allow us to sell items individually but also let the customer put together bundles of items or create their own packages (for example, choosing multiple items to comprise a gift basket)

Knowing that Companies A and D are our contenders, we can now look at the specifications that their respective e-commerce packages offer. Let's assume their advertisements and sales representatives provide us with the following information:

Company A:
Secure Cart
Supports up to 5000 items
Online Auction Support
Supports Credit Cards
Supports E-Checks
Supports Gift Certificates
Supports Mail-in Payments
Can Sell Individual Items
Foreign Currency Support

Company D:
Secure Cart
Supports up to 2000 items
Supports Credit Cards
Supports E-Checks
Supports Gift Certificates
Can Sell Individual Items
Can Sell Bundled Items

In our Shopping Cart Feature Table, we first list the specifications for Company A, then for Company D. If there is an exact duplicate (such as "Secure Cart"), it is okay to list the specification one time to represent both companies A and D.

Shopping Cart and Catalog		Companies	
		Company A	Company D
Specifications	Secure Cart	√	√
	Up to 5000 Items	√	
	Online Auction Support	√	
	Credit Card Support	√	√
	E-Check Support	√	√
	Gift Certificate Support	√	√
	Mail-in Payment Support	√	
	Can Sell Individual Items	√	√
	Foreign Currency Support	√	
	Up to 2000 Items	√	√
	Can Sell Bundled Items		√

Feature Table (Shopping Cart and Catalog)

As you can see from the *Shopping Cart and Catalog* Feature Table, all of the unique specifications are listed without redundancy. Although Company D offers many of the same features as Company A, we've listed each feature only once. Notice that Company A's support of up to 5000 items includes the subset of 2000 items of Company D's catalog, but our requirement is not expected to exceed 500 items.

Now, let's eliminate the "fluff." Using the table we just created, we will eliminate the details that are unrelated to our requirements. The process of elimination will keep us focused on what is important to our business and prevent us from being oversold on a solution.

In our example, we don't need online auction support, mail-in payment capability, or foreign currency support.

Shopping Cart and Catalog	Companies	
	Company A	Company D
Secure Cart	√	√
Up to 5000 Items	√	
Online Auction Support	√	
Credit Card Support	√	√
E-Check Support	√	√
Gift Certificate Support	√	√
Mail-in Payment Support	√	
Can Sell Individual Items	√	√
Foreign Currency Support	√	
Up to 2000 Items	√	√
Can Sell Bundled Items		√

Feature Table (Shopping Cart and Catalog)

We can also remove any duplicated functionality in excess of our needs, which in this case would be the support for up to 5000 catalog items.

With our updated list, we can now evaluate which company is best able to meet our actual needs by placing check marks in the columns next to each required specification. After adjusting the table to reflect what we need, the decision making process becomes significantly easier.

Shopping Cart and Catalog		Companies	
		Company A	Company D
Specifications	Secure Cart	√	√
	Credit Card Support	√	√
	E-Check Support	√	√
	Gift Certificate Support	√	√
	Can Sell Individual Items	√	√
	Up to 2000 Items	√	√
	Can Sell Bundled Items		√

Updated Feature Table (Shopping Cart and Catalog)

In this case, Company D is the only one that meets all of our requirements, even though Company A touted some impressive bells & whistles and more features overall. Even if Company A offered all of the *extras* at a cost savings over Company D, the absence of *bundled item support* made Company A's package insufficient for us.

In more complex tables where several companies seem to meet your needs, or where there is no single company that completely satisfies all of your preferences, you can replace the check marks with numeric scores to indicate the relative priority of a feature or specification. The following scale is useful for your analysis:

n/a – Not offered / Not applicable
0 – Not important
1 – Important / Preferred
2 – Very Important / Essential

After assigning values to each specification, you can add the values in each column and determine the best fit from the available selections. The column with the highest value is *likely* to be your best option.

We'll illustrate by revisiting the original feature table shown on page 137. When we assign numbers to score the specifications, Company D is still our best option as indicated in the table below. If you are considering multiple companies and several end up with the same total score, change the above scale from 0, 1, and 2, respectively, to 0, 2, and 4.

Shopping Cart and Catalog		Companies	
		Company A	Company D
	Secure Cart	2	2
	Up to 5000 Items	1	n/a
	Online Auction Support	0	n/a
	Credit Card Support	2	2
	E-Check Support	2	2
Specifications	Gift Certificate Support	2	2
	Mail-in Payment Support	0	n/a
	Can Sell Individual Items	2	2
	Foreign Currency Support	0	n/a
	Up to 2000 Items	2	2
	Can Sell Bundled Items	n/a	2
	TOTAL SCORE	13	14

Feature Table (Shopping Cart and Catalog) evaluated with numeric scores instead of check marks.

If you do not use the objective decision methods suggested in this book, come up with something on your own that works well for you. The key is to take emotion out of the decision-making process as you consider your options.

More than eighty percent of sales are based on an emotional response, whether it is from a convincing sales demonstration or a fear of loss in "limited time only" ads. We have all been *sold to* at one point or another. A skilled salesperson knows all of the right questions to ask and is deftly able to match your answers with the features and benefits offered by their product or service. It's nothing to get upset about—they're just doing their job, and if they believe in what they sell, they are probably passionate about why theirs is the best on the market. In most cases, no one is trying to deceive you or misrepresent what they sell.

Your role in the sale is to be a well-informed consumer. Collect all of the available information and evaluate it to make the best buying decision for your business. After hearing a few sales presentations or reading dozens of descriptions from various software packages, it becomes difficult to keep all of the information sorted out. Prioritizing the details becomes even more challenging if you do not have an effective system to help you make decisions.

If you approach the decision process systematically, you are less likely to be swayed by extras that are cost-added versus value-added. Being analytical may add time to the front end of your shopping experience, but ultimately you will save a substantial amount of time avoiding the confusing (and sometimes agonizing) task of providing your business with the right solution for success.

Asking questions and making decisions:

- Take the time to define your requirements by asking yourself what your Website should do.

- Use a prioritization system to list what is most to least important then eliminate companies that can not provide what you need.

- If you start with pros and cons on paper, the process of deciding on a solution becomes easier because it is more rational and less emotional.

- View sample portfolio sites and obtain detailed information (or a consultation) from the provider(s) you feel are most qualified.

Section Five: Marketing

Topics Covered:

Creating a Good Return on Investment

Marketing through Search Engines

and

User-Friendliness in Marketing

Earning a Return on Investment (ROI)

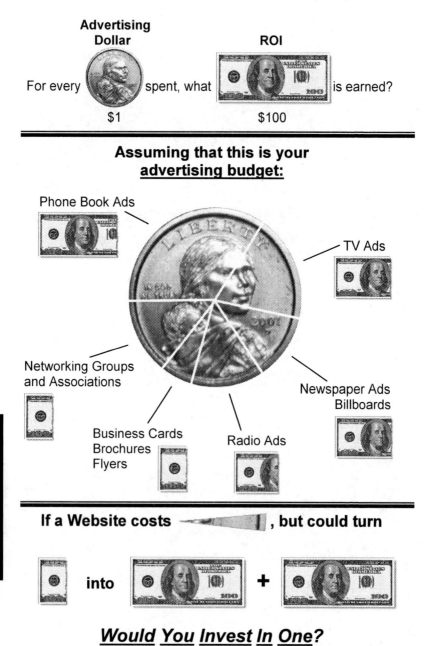

Advertising Dollar

ROI

For every $1 spent, what $100 is earned?

Assuming that this is your advertising budget:

Phone Book Ads

TV Ads

Networking Groups and Associations

Newspaper Ads
Billboards

Business Cards
Brochures
Flyers

Radio Ads

If a Website costs , **but could turn**

into **+**

Would You Invest In One?

144

Creating a Good Return on Investment

Choosing Your Website's Domain Name
(Your "www" Address)

Your domain name is the Web address that you will use to "brand" your Website. You should register a unique domain name for your Website as soon as you decide to establish your business online. Your domain name will likely be something similar to your business name or indicative of the products and services that you sell. It is actually your *domain name* that you will promote to the general public, as people will find your Website by typing your domain name into their Internet browsers.

Your domain name should be short and easy to remember. Long domain names with tricky spellings or plays on words are ineffective because they can confuse your customers. For example, if you owned a shoe repair service called "Shoes Heel Sew Fast," the name may seem clever on a business card, but for Website purposes, your identity can get lost in the spelling:

Hmmm. Was it www.shoesheelsewfast.com?
Or www.shoeshealsewfast.com?
Or www.shoeshealsofast.com?
Or www.shoesheelsofast.com?
Or was it a .net, .biz, or some other type of domain name instead of a .com?

Notice that once the spaces are removed from the business name (the Internet doesn't allow spaces in domain names) the cuteness goes away. The resulting string of letters becomes confusing.

Also, even more important, take the time to write out any domain name you are thinking of selecting to make sure that the end result does not have an unintended "double meaning." Domain names do not use spacing or capitalization and are limited to hyphens when using symbols. Selecting a domain name made of more than one word can spell disaster for your organization's identity and public image if you're not careful. Unless it is done intentionally for effect, double-meanings that come from combined words will probably not serve your purpose well.

For example, if your business were an art appreciation gallery called "Union of Art", and you wanted to use the company name as your domain name, the resulting domain could conceivably be www.unionofart.com. The domain name, itself, could be easily confused with topics other than *art*, given how the human eye inserts natural breaks in the name.

In a more dramatic example of a name that may be easily misinterpreted or misread, a hypothetical news service named "Your News Exchange" registered as www.yournewsexchange.com may not reach its intended audience. Would people read it as YourNewsExchange.com or would they see YourNewSexChange.com? The general public won't intuitively know what to think.

Is there anything *wrong* with double-meaning names? Not necessarily. There is an element of publicity that a clever play on words can yield in such cases. Nonetheless, put some thought into your domain name and look at it on paper before finalizing your decision to create your online identity.

Email and Reciprocal Links to Your Site

Surprisingly, there are some simple ways to promote your Website (domain name) at no expense at all. For starters, you can add a link to your Website in the signature block of each email that you send. As you contact more people on a regular basis, and in turn, as they forward your emails to other interested parties, your domain name will make its way around the Internet from person to person. Out of curiosity or by your suggestion, people will click on the domain name link to your Website from your emails, and the traffic to your site will favorably impact your Website's popularity.

Also, having your domain name linked from other sites will help drive traffic your way. It can take some time to negotiate adding your link to another Website, but polite requests and good people skills in asking the Webmaster of other sites will often get the results you want. Offering to reciprocate the favor by adding a link to their Website from yours makes it easier, too.

Printed Materials

Another effortless way to market your site is to include your domain name on every printed form of advertisement that already represents your business. True, telephone book ads, business cards, stationery, catalogs, brochures, etc. all bear some expense, but if you are paying for them anyway (independent of owning a Website), then adding your domain name to your advertising literature imposes no additional or appreciable costs to your business.

Marketing

Broadcasting

If your business uses broadcasting methods of advertisement (TV, radio, etc.), you can simply add a boost for your site on the tail end of such advertisements by mentioning your domain name in a quick "Check us out online at www.yourbusiness.com" blurb. It will stand out to people if it is the last thing they hear, and they will remember your domain name easier than they will remember your phone number.

Emblematic Promotional Items

Many companies use emblematic items branded with their logos to promote business: pens, key chains, calendars, note pads, and more. Put your domain name on the promotional items that you hand out to clients, visitors, and guests.

Business Card-Size CD-ROMs

At a nominal expense, you can even have your business cards printed onto business card-size CD-ROMs that your clients can insert into their computers. Curiosity usually drives people to investigate what is on the CD, and if the disc brings up a page with a link to your Website, you'll find that Web traffic comes your way almost overnight.

Text Message Campaigns

Text message marketing is becoming the new trend in driving traffic to Websites. Most people carry cellular phones today, and "texting" people has become an abridged version of sending emails to each other via cell phone. If you locate and use a text messaging service that relays traffic to your Website, this new trend in advertisement can be one of the most powerful ways to reach people. Text messaging campaigns can provide powerful and instantaneous access to your Website from mobile users.

Pay-Per-Click and Subscribed Links

Pay-per-click and subscribed links are two ways of promoting your Website directly on the search engines. They position your Website in search engine rankings based on how much you pay for particular keywords or placement. On the search results, a portion of the screen is reserved for these two types of paid-for advertisements, usually on top of the screen or in the right margin.

On the plus side, your site can be prominently found by people who search for the specific combination of keywords that you pay to list. On the minus side, the costs can add up quickly. Also, Internet security software often treats the paid-for ads as adware (or spam) and prevents them from being displayed, and viewers often ignore paid-for links the same way they would avoid reading through junk mail.

Paid-for advertisement also has another drawback. If your competition wants to run up your bill on a pay-per-click link, they can essentially torpedo your advertising budget by employing other-than-ethical tactics to visiting your site on your dime... or quarter... or dollar... or *more* per click. The business with a tight advertising budget should probably steer clear of pay-per-click or subscribed link advertising.

Marketing

Marketing through Search Engines

Search Engines are one of the most misunderstood pieces of Website solutions. They are so simple to use when we go online to find something, so the assumption that many Website owners make is that they are simple to figure out in terms of getting their Website found or listed in search rankings. Not true.

This section is not intended to make you a Search Engine Optimization (SEO) or Search Engine Marketing (SEM) expert. In fact, without devoting dozens of hours each month to the topic, it would be impossible to be considered an expert in either. But in just a few minutes of reading, you *can* develop a good understanding of things that must be considered in your Website's design so you know what to look for when approaching a Website solution provider.

In the previous section, we discussed paid-for placement on the search engines. Aside from the area of a search engine listings page that displays paid-for results, most of the page is used to display *natural* search engine rankings. Natural search engine rankings are those that result from three criteria that we'll explore in this section: Text, Links, and Traffic.

First and foremost, understand that nobody, and I mean *nobody,* can ethically guarantee or promise that you will achieve the Number One spot in any natural search engine ranking. It's just not realistic. Think about it. How many Website owners want the Number One spot? All of them. And how many Web development companies would tell you that they're 2nd best? None. So to earn your business, it is sometimes alluring for a developer to make such a promise (that you'll get the number one spot) knowing that time is on their side, and once your bill is paid for the site, a token partial refund for non-delivery on an SEO guarantee would still result in a net profit for the developer on the sale of the site.

Most developers do not operate in such a shady way, but if you approach one that makes empty promises about "guaranteed" placement in a natural search engine ranking, beware. Forewarned is forearmed.

Search Engines versus Directories

In casual conversation, it is common to hear people talking about browsing the Web or doing a search for one thing or another on the Internet. In the same context, you may hear the term *Search Engine* used as well. People refer to search engines as the online tools that help them find (search for) information or products using particular topics or words (called *keywords*). When you hear people refer to "the search engines," they are categorically referring to such sites as Google™ search (www.google.com), Yahoo!® search (www.yahoo.com), MSN® search (www.msn.com), and others that offer keyword search services.

In actuality, the sites that are used to search for information on the Internet can be divided into two types: search engines and directories. There are several differences with regard to how information is indexed (or *ranked*) between search engines and directories, but when it comes to looking for something on the Web, they are treated interchangeably from a consumer's standpoint.

151

Search engines, Google for example, use computer programs to evaluate and index Websites. Directories like Yahoo!, on the other hand, involve human beings in evaluating, categorizing, and ranking Websites that have been submitted for review. In both cases there are numerous criteria used to determine where a Website falls within the ranked listings. The criteria used to rank sites vary between each search service and change on a monthly basis.

This is what makes SEO a *moving target* and explains why SEO has become an industry unto itself. It is much more effective to hire an SEO company to work with your site than to do it yourself (unless *you* are already an expert in the field).

For your Website to be found by a customer who uses the search service sites, your site's design must be periodically modified to consider the elements used by search engines and directories. The process of making the necessary changes to your site's design to enhance its position in the rankings is called Search Engine Optimization (SEO).

Understanding SEO Criteria

Search Engine Optimization has become a specialty among some Internet solution providers. The task of optimizing a Website is very challenging because individual search services place different emphasis on SEO elements.

Search services score sites based on three basic groups of data: the quality and relevance of text on a Website, the quality and nature of links to and from a Website, and the amount of traffic that visits a

Website. There is favorable consideration given to well-constructed sites using these factors, and there can be penalization in placement (or even complete omission) on the search services for poor or inappropriate site designs.

Your search for the right Website solution should include questions about a company's SEO services, costs, and experience.

Text Criteria

Meta-data is the term used to describe displayed and non-displayed textual properties of your Website used in optimizing it for the search engines. The information in your meta-data is contained within the programming code of your Website. Your site's page titles, keywords, and descriptions are examples of meta-data. Most of it is not shown on the screen when a visitor views your site, but search engines evaluate all of it to determine your site's rankings.

Text on Web Pages

The text on your Website is important. It should be well thought out and relevant to the purpose of the site. Search engines and directories consider the quality of the text on your site when determining how your site is ranked.

Quality of Text and Meta-Data

The quality of your text refers to its relevance with the site description, keywords, and page titles used in the meta-data. If the text is relevant to your topic and contains matches to your site's meta-data, it is considered better quality than if it is completely unrelated.

To give an example, let's assume that your site advertises automotive products, and your keywords include various brands and manufacturers by name. Good quality text would feature those same brands and manufacturers in the body of the page. On the other hand, using the keywords of "sex, drugs, and rock & roll" on the same site to appeal to mass traffic on the Internet would be considered poor quality due to the lack of relevance to the content of the site.

Text quality and meta-data quality also relate to the types of words used within the site. Adjectives and other "flowery language" lack quality and relevance that specific nouns or verbs contribute to a site's content.

Text Placement

The location of text on a page is also important to the relevance between content and meta-data. If keywords are mentioned early, near the top of a page, they are considered more important to a search than if they are found lower towards the bottom of the page. If they are mentioned more than once on the page, and as long as they are not *overused*, the weighting of keyword relevance is higher than if a word is used only one time.

Text Characteristics

Search engine ranking criteria go as far as to consider the size and typesetting of words used in the content of a Web page. Bold and italicized words are treated with priority over normal text, and if a word is typeset in a different color, font, or point-size to make it stand out from surrounding words, so much the better.

Descriptions, Titles, Alt-Tags

Each Web page can and should be given a unique description and title. For Website visitors with slower connections, each picture on a page can be assigned alternative labels called *Alt-Tags* to distinguish them as the page is loaded in the visitor's browser.

A site that is properly optimized for search engines will include specific words in the descriptions, titles, and Alt-Tags that correspond to keywords on the page. Search engines evaluate the quality and relevance of these elements in the bigger picture of ranking the site against other Websites using the same or similar keywords. Therefore, do not have a Home Page with a generic page title of *Home* but one that is more descriptive of your business.

Flash Limitations

Flash animation is a feature that combines text, pictures, sound, and other forms of multimedia. Adding Flash to Web pages gives a Website a nice flair and eye-catching appeal. However, there are some general drawbacks to *over-using* Flash on a site, using Flash to link pages within a site, or creating the site entirely with Flash. Not all programs that create Flash do so in ways that are search engine "friendly."

Remember our discussion about keyword relevance to text on the site and that search engines evaluate the quality of the text characteristics. When text is animated using Flash, the text content is first converted to a picture. So in the finished product, the text that you see moving around on the screen is not actually text, but images of text that Flash manipulates on the screen. Unfortunately, search engines do not interpret images as having any relevance to keywords, so the site can become search engine *unfriendly*.

In much the same way, links from one page to another via buttons or navigation menus made with some versions of Flash are unreadable by search engines. As a result, a site created *entirely* in Flash may be interpreted as a single Web page with no searchable links or content, and the result is that the site may never get found in a natural ranking with some search engines.

There are ways to combine the use of Flash with more traditional programming on a Website so your site can have the best of both worlds: effective searchable content and captivating multimedia effects. Be sure that your Web developer is well-versed in keeping the balance between *effect* and *effectiveness*. If you are building your own site, get familiar with these important considerations as well.

Link Criteria

The second set of criteria evaluated by search engines and directories is links. Links connect Web pages to other Websites or Web pages. Depending on how they are used, they are considered a form of advertising or promotion for the destination (target) page or site. Think of links on other sites that connect to your site as a referral to your business.

When search engines rank a site, they index it based on the site's content. Using programs affectionately called *Web bots* (Web robots) or *Spiders*, search engines "crawl" the Web and follow the links that are found with each Website's content. As other sites are indexed, their links are followed as well. Search engines spend their time following the connections from links to links across the World Wide Web. In the end, the more links around the World Wide Web that point to your site, the more prominent your site's ranking becomes in search results due to its link popularity and promotion.

Developed-by Links

If you look at the bottom of many Websites created by traditional designers, you will notice links that lead back to the company that developed the site. There is nothing inherently *wrong* with this, but you should be aware of why this is a common practice.

At first thought, you might consider that it is giving credit where credit is due. True enough. The implications, however, go much deeper from a search engine perspective. Recall that the more links that point to a site, the more popular the site becomes and the higher the potential placement in the search engine rankings. Using this insight, a Web developer often adds links to their site on the sites they produce, thus creating multiple links to their own site via their clients.

As a result, *your* site becomes part of your developer's search engine optimization strategy for their own site. To make this a mutual benefit, request that they include a reciprocal link from their site to yours as part of their online portfolio. After all, the relationship between you and your developer should be a symbiotic relationship, not a parasitic relationship that only benefits one side (them).

Reciprocal Links

Establishing reciprocal links is a great way to start promoting your Website while supporting businesses with whom you have (or want to have) a relationship.

For example, a real estate agent may want a Web page focused on relocation services for anyone moving into the area. The page could include links to utility companies, school systems, and mortgage lenders. In exchange, the Webmasters who manage the sites where those links point to may be willing to add links to the real estate agent's site.

In the end, more links pointing to your site help drive traffic to your site. Becoming a central point that links to other useful sites adds value for your visitors and can increase your site's popularity. Consider quality link exchanges with sites that have content and articles relevant to yours to be a good way of promoting your business while improving your search engine rankings.

Broken Links

We've discussed many ways to use links on your site to improve positioning in the search engine rankings. *Broken links*, on the other hand, will significantly degrade your search engine position.

A broken link is simply one that points to a page or content that doesn't exist. If the broken link is supposed to point to another site or a different page on your site, the resulting screen will display "Page Not Found" or another message indicating that the link was invalid. If the broken link is supposed to display a picture or other item on a page, a small red "X" (or similar emblem) displays, indicating that the item cannot be found.

In any case, when your site is indexed for search engine placement, broken links are viewed unfavorably. The search engines and directories consider broken links an indicator of inattention to detail and a poorly managed Website.

There are two primary reasons that broken links may appear on a site. The first is careless spelling when defining the link while creating the Website. Your developer should catch those types of errors during the design and usability testing process.

The second reason a broken link may appear is that the target site, page, or element referenced by the link becomes changed, removed, or replaced. If your site links to other sites (or uses linked pictures, forms, or documents on other sites), and if the site administrator of the target site deletes or changes the filenames, page names, or so on, then the link that is used *on your site* will no longer be valid. Instead of displaying the intended image, element, or object, the broken link symbol will appear on the screen. As a result, your search engine standing suffers.

Due to the fact that you probably do not have management control of the sites that your Website links to, you need to frequently review your site for inconsistencies and broken links that may have previously been intact. If you are paying a Web developer to manage your site, this is something that they may do as part of the monthly hosting and management fee.

Traffic Criteria

The final "biggie" in determining search engine placement is your site's traffic popularity. Of course, when you first establish your online presence, your popularity is zero. You've had no traffic. But as people begin finding your site through keyword relevant searches and visitors linking from other Websites, your site should begin to see more and more traffic.

An aggressive marketing campaign that drives people to visit your site through exposure and awareness will help your popularity even more. The more Web traffic that your site experiences, the higher your ranking will become. Eventually your site can become in such demand that the traffic component of search engine criteria affects your ranking more than the text criteria.

At the point which your site is popularized by traffic-hits-per-keyword more so than by text-relevance-per-keyword, you might decide to experiment more with Flash-based multimedia pages. At that point, your search engine profile has become much more solid by *popular demand*.

A Final Word on Search Engine Ranking "Guarantees"

Most companies that have been around for many years are reputable, but it bears repeating that you must be leery of anyone who guarantees a specific natural (also called *organic*) positioning *with or without* a money back provision if they are unsuccessful in achieving the promised results. Why? *Because no such guarantees are valid!*

A methodical analysis and consistent review of your SEO strategy should gradually elevate your placement to optimal levels. It may take days, weeks, or months for a given keyword to reflect your placement on the first page of search results. Your search results depend on individual words used, and some keywords may not yield favorable or desirable results at all. The company that performs your SEO action plan should have the tools, knowledge, and experience to research your keyword choices and assess their merit in terms of optimizing your site.

Know what is involved with Search Engine Optimization when you set out to find an SEO service provider. Be familiar with the limitations of pay-per-click and subscribed links, as well as why no online solutions company can guarantee your natural ranking on the search engines. In general, the best overall plan is to optimize your site using effective practices through a consistent, methodical strategy.

Usability

Website *user friendliness* has become increasingly important over the past few years. You may have a very attractive Website design, and the site may have been optimized to show up prominently in the search engines. If, however, your visitors can not find what they want on it, or if navigating your site is too hard, they will click their browser's *Back* button and simply move on to your competition, never to return. The focus on your Website's user friendliness is known as Website *usability*, and it is a key component in Website development.

Web Aesthetics

One of the more basic elements of usability includes the artistic orientation of the site. Websites that have been assembled using dithered (dotted) or pixilated (jagged, blocky) pictures obviously do not display well. They do not convey a professional impression to Website visitors. Likewise, mismatched image types (cartoon clipart mixed with professional photographs), uncoordinated colors (clashing), and so forth make for a poorly constructed Website design.

You may have more pictures in your portfolio or from your digital camera than you should put on your Website. You may even have some clipart images that you want to display on your site, but be careful about mixing the two haphazardly. Whereas it may be fine to show pictures of products that you sell along with the clipart of major credit cards that you accept, it doesn't look good to place elegant portfolio photos on the same page as animated cartoons or poorly scanned images.

Regarding the overall site layout, a professional contemporary design should have a crisp look with clean lines and curves. In the late 1990's, backgrounds with busy patterns, boxy buttons, large fonts, and randomly-placed advertising banners were commonplace. Improvements in Website technology have brought about changes. Fly-out & dropdown menus, smoothly transitioning slide shows, and image drop-shadows (offset lighting effect that gives pictures a 3-dimensional perspective) on a clean or subtle background are prevalent and preferred today.

Clicks to Destination

The number of clicks it takes to arrive at a particular page (*click-throughs*) is a major usability consideration. In general a maximum of three click-throughs should be allowed. In other words, if your visitor needs to click on more than three buttons or links to find what they want on the site, the site should be adjusted to reduce the path required to get to the destination. Too many clicks (more than three) means that the site's navigation is too confusing and your visitors will have a tendency to get "lost" within the pages.

Unlike a printed textbook or magazine where a reader can flip back and forth and hold their place with their thumb, Websites are intangible representations of physical pages. People lose their place more easily when there are no physical reference points. Excessive scrolling (up and down) and clicking on links that jump from page to page compounds the problem, and visitors perceive that they have to dig too much to find what they want. If it's too inconvenient, they go elsewhere.

Marketing

Multimedia

Music, sound, video, and animations are all parts of multimedia. Effective use of multimedia components on your Website can captivate attention and significantly enhance a visitor's browsing experience. However, ineffective use of multimedia leads to confusion and detracts from the quality of your site.

When you have sound, video, Flash, or other multimedia on your Website, you may want it to be activated upon a click from your visitors rather than have it start automatically when they view the page. If you do decide to have the feature play automatically, only have it play one time rather than allowing it to loop indefinitely. Most visitors appreciate the control of being able to play it on demand instead of having it forced upon them.

Quality becomes a big factor with sound and video on your site. An otherwise professional looking site can be significantly devalued by putting distorted or poorly edited home-video images on a page. If the video has not been edited and adjusted to have a professional edge, do not post it on your site. Likewise, if your music or sound quality is muffled or distorted, don't post it. It is better to omit a rough element now and post it later when it is refined. Do not compromise the quality of your site just to have more bells and whistles in its design.

Text Congestion

Books are meant to be read. Websites are meant to be experienced. Viewing a Website should not be a cumbersome process that requires your customers to *study*. Excessive text bogs down your site and can give the site an unbalanced, heavy, or even boring appearance.

There should be enough text on the site to be relevant to search engines, informative and interesting, but not overwhelming. If you have a lot of material to convey, perhaps for research purposes, then it is better to create a *link page* (library style) or database on your site where the information can be downloaded or displayed selectively on demand. Leave the main pages of your site simple enough to be user friendly to your visitors.

Consistency in Theme

As we've discussed, it can be more confusing for your customers to navigate a Website than to thumb around in a book. To make your visitors more comfortable, ensure that your site has a similar theme or appearance from page to page in terms of layout.

Content will differ from one page to the next on your site as it does in a book or magazine. However, if a person loses his or her place in a book that they're *holding*, they at least know that they're still in the same book. Your Website visitors should never arrive at a page and be left wondering if they're still on the same site. A consistent theme will help them keep their bearings if they lose their place online.

Site Maps and Bread Crumbs- Quick Reference

One last element of usability to be address is the use of a site map. A site map is basically an organized listing of your site with pages arranged by category for easy navigation. Your visitors can display the site map and see an overview of your site, much like a table of contents. It should be accessible from any page on the site, just in case someone gets lost and wants to reach a central point of navigation.

To enhance the user friendliness of a site, consider supplementing your site map by adding *bread crumbs* to your Web pages. Bread crumbs are a series of navigation links that make it easier for your visitor to find their way back from whence they came. For example, if you own a landscaping company and a Website visitor links from your Home Page to a Services Page, and then clicks on a page called Pressed Concrete, they may see a set of bread crumb links on top of the page as follows:

Home>>Services>>Pressed Concrete

Search engines like site maps and bread crumbs and will often favor a site that is built with such usability considerations.

To get your best return on investment:

- Choose a domain name carefully, write it down, and evaluate it on paper before registering it.

- Take advantage of free or inexpensive promotion opportunities that are available.

- Keep text, link, and traffic considerations in mind when defining the content of each Web page.

- Keep your customers coming back by paying particular attention to the user-friendliness of your Website.

Section Six: Your Next Step

Topics Covered:

Furthering Your Education

and

Wrapping It Up

The Internet Business Cycle

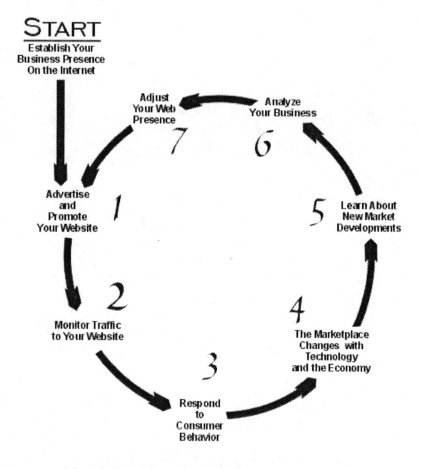

Like a brick-and-mortar business, you must continually review, improve, and promote your Web presence.

Get Educated and Focused

You're not done. You're *never* done! Whether you already have a Web presence or are ready to take the first steps to get started with one, your work is far from over. Much like any form of advertising, doing business online requires continued attention and adjustment. The Internet is a dynamic canvas on which you paint your business, but as technology changes, your online presence must adapt as well.

Now that you are more aware of how establishing a Web presence can benefit your business, and perhaps you know more about how you would like to represent your business on the Internet, your next step is to familiarize yourself with the various resources that are available to you as you move forward.

There are many sources of information available online regarding Website solutions. Visit the Learning Center page on ***www.WebDrafter.com*** or check the search engines for Web development companies in your local area. You will find that many Web developers offer free classes or seminars on the topics of *Web design* and *choosing a service provider*. Be aware that most of them will not be completely unbiased as they guide you towards a decision. After all, there is something in it for them to earn your business at their free seminars.

Many developers have pages of valuable information on their Websites. Some even post Webinars (online seminars) to help you learn more. The Learning Center page of *www.WebDrafter.com* contains a Webinar that will help you determine what you need, what to expect, and how to approach your Website solution provider. Whether you build a site yourself,

169

use a turnkey solution, or find a developer to do the work for you, making an informed decision is much more cost effective than being spontaneous when your business is concerned.

Also, visit **www.Website411Book.com** for bonus materials and helpful resources related to establishing a successful business on the Internet. You will find an informational database of Website solution providers in various cities across the country, including the services they provide. For access to the *free* bonus materials (only available to people who have this book), enter the following *case-sensitive* information at the login prompt:

Username: website
Password: 411

In addition to a database of Web solution providers near you, the bonus section includes useful links, a help forum, business tools, checklists to help you decide upon the right solution, multimedia presentations to help you learn, and much more.

Learn more about Websites, merchant accounts, search engines, and other resources available for promoting your business by sending a text message from your cell phone. Simply text the word **website411book** to the abbreviated phone number 62898. When you send *website411book* to the five-digit phone number (62898), you will automatically receive a reply with more information.

Not only will doing so provide you with more information, but it will also serve as a *live demonstration* of how text message marketing works (as discussed in the Marketing section of this book)!

As you continue your research on the topic of Websites, make a concerted effort to spend a few hours getting more familiar with the basics. Insist that any company that provides you with information explains it in understandable terms, not technical jargon. Most importantly, don't allow anyone to pressure you into limited-time offers or last-chance deals.

Take advantage of sales and promotional specials, but if you need time to think about the details, your Web developer should be able to honor their offer after you have had time to "sleep on it." Most reputable companies won't use "now or never" pressure tactics to capture your wallet.

Once you decide on a solution, don't delay in getting started with the design process. If you intend to do the work yourself, plan on making your Website a focal point for several weeks, a little each day, so that you don't lose continuity between your ideas. It is easier to knock out the project at one time than it is to spread the design intermittently over several months.

Be consistent in making progress daily, but also be careful not to rush through the project just to get it put behind you. Remember, quality and usability matter to your customers. The site must add value to their experience with you.

If you are hiring a developer to do the work, collect all of your information, photos, documents, videos, brochures, and so on prior to the project start date.

Providing all of the files and information up front will save you time and expense.

Every delay that the developer experiences in obtaining your information costs you money because they have to regroup, refocus, refamiliarize, and get back "in the groove" with your project each time they put it aside to await materials from you. Those delays easily translate to hundreds of dollars in extra hourly costs. Good and frequent communication is the key to a successful, cost-effective project.

As you make your decision:

🖱 Reputable companies will allow you time to shop around and may even make no-risk, try-before-you-buy offers.

☺ Some developers offer incentives, specials, discounts, or benefits for customer loyalty. Inquire about them as you do your research.

☠ Shy away from high-pressure, on-the-spot decisions, "now or never" deals, or warnings of higher prices "if you don't act now."

Wrapping It Up

Does *your* business need a Web presence? If you have read this book cover to cover, then you have enough solid information to make an informed decision about doing business online. The next step is yours.

Expanding your business onto the Internet may be new to you. You may have previously thought a Website to be an additional, unnecessary expense. Perhaps you have simply resigned yourself to the fact that having one is now more of a necessity than a novelty. In any case, you probably use the Web to do your own research, unwittingly contributing to the recent changes in consumer trends and shopping habits.

Whether you view a Website as *cutting edge* or as a *necessary evil*, there's no arguing that more people are turning to the online economy each month. If you think of a Web presence as simply the online counterpart to your traditional business, then getting established on the Internet isn't such a formidable process.

Ask your Web developer to speak to you in layman's terms. Programmers and Web designers work in an environment of acronyms and "alphabet soup" jargon day in and day out, talking in cryptic terms like *HTML, pixels, megabytes,* and so forth. Sometimes they take it for granted that the rest of the world understands the techno-babble that is common in the Website industry.

Be comfortable asking them to slow down, rephrase, and use plain language in communicating their ideas for your project. Interview them before you get started. Use this book as a good source of questions to ask. Your Website development experience should be interactive and understandable by both you *and* your solution provider. If it's not, then stop, regroup, and find a solution provider, turnkey package, or consultant that meets you on your terms and at your comfort level.

Listen to your Web developer's guidance which comes from their experience of working with many projects and clientele. Consider their advice, and temper it with your goals and vision for your company's or organization's identity. If something doesn't seem to fit, don't force it; clarify, ask why, and then make an executive decision to go forward in the direction that best meets your needs.

You are the boss. You have the big picture. Make sure that you know what to expect from your Web solution, and you will find that an effective Web presence will "complete" your business in today's marketplace.

A personal note to *YOU* as you venture forward

On a time-permitting basis, I do my best to answer all emails that I receive. If you have Website questions about the subject matter contained within my book, please feel free to send them to me at TomElliott@Website411Book.com. I will do my best to reply in a timely manner. In the meantime, best of good fortune to you!

Sincerely,

Author

Your Next Step

Acknowledgements

Acknowledgements

In writing this book, I communicated with more than 500 Website companies. Of the solution providers I visited or reviewed online, I received communications via email in the form of price quotes, estimates, advice, consultations, and various other correspondence from over 400 companies that were used to validate, calculate, and confirm the information and opinions expressed in this text.

I express special thanks to Karen Elliott, Melodi Elliott, Thomas P. Elliott, Faye Hetrick, David Moskowitz, Eric Parish, and James B. Troutman for their unselfish help and patience in reviewing, editing, and shaping this book.

References and Recommended Reading

"Frequently Asked Questions." Small Business Administration Office of Advocacy. <http://www.sba.gov/advo/stats/sbfaq.pdf>

Headd, Brian. "Redefining Business Success: Distinguishing Between Closure and Failure." *Small Business Economics,* 21.1 (August 2003): 51-61.

Knaup, Amy E. "Survival and Longevity in the Business Employment Dynamics Database." *Monthly Labor Review,* 128. 5 (May 2005): 50-6.

Krug, Steve. *Don't Make Me Think: A Common Sense Approach to Web Usability, 2nd Edition.* Indianapolis, IN: New Riders Publishing, 2005.

Moran, Mike. *Do It Wrong Quickly: How the Web Changes the Old Marketing Rules.* Boston, MA: Pearson Education, Inc., 2008.

"Nearly 80 Percent of U.S. Adults Go Online." c|net News. Reuters. 5 Nov. 2007. <http://www.news.com/Nearly-80-percent-of-U.S.-adults-go-online/2100-1038_3-6217159.html>

Nielsen, Jakob, and Marie Tahir. *Homepage Usability: 50 Websites Deconstructed.* Indianapolis, IN: New Riders Publishing, 2002.

"paradigm." *Dictionary.com Unabridged (v 1.1).* Random House, Inc. 21 Jul. 2007.

"paradigm." *The American Heritage® Dictionary of the English Language, Fourth Edition.* Houghton Mifflin Company, 2004. 21 Jul. 2007.

"paradigm shift." *Webster's New Millennium™ Dictionary of English, Preview Edition (v 0.9.7).* Lexico Publishing Group, LLC. 21 Jul. 2007.

Rawlinson, G. E. *The Significance of Letter Position in Word Recognition.* Unpublished PhD Thesis, Psychology Department, University of Nottingham, Nottingham UK, 1976.

Shillcock, R., Ellison, T.M. & Monaghan, P. "Eye-Fixation Behaviour, Lexical Storage and Visual Word Recognition in a Split Processing Model." *Psychological Review.* (2000): 107, 824-851.

Thurow, Shari. *Search Engine Visibility.* Indianapolis, IN: New Riders Publishing, 2003.

Index

Index

189

Notes:

Notes:

Notes:

About the Author

Tom Elliott is a native of Arlington, Massachusetts, born in 1968. After graduating with a bachelors degree from Purdue University, he was commissioned as a Naval officer in 1990 where he served aboard submarines and aircraft carriers.

While in the Navy, Tom started a computer business in 1992. The business was portable as he moved from duty station to duty station, focusing on hardware and network consulting. In 2000, he shifted from a concentration on hardware to Website design and began WebDrafter.com, Inc. After much success and expansion into the Internet environment, Tom became concurrently involved with (and was recognized as the 2002 Certified Internet Trainer of the Year for) a North Carolina based Internet marketing company and was subsequently invited to an Internet Advisory Board position. He joined their corporate team in 2003 as the Director of Internet Training and Sales after resigning his commission in the military 13 years into his 20-year career. Then in 2005, he resigned from the corporate environment in North Carolina to focus on expanding WebDrafter.com, Inc. on a full-time basis.

In 2005 he earned his Master's of Science Degree in Information Systems from the Florida Institute of Technology. His other business affiliations have included serving on the Board of Directors for the Better Business Bureau of Central North Carolina, the Bachelor Degree Program Advisory Board of ECPI School of Technology in Virginia Beach, VA, and Advisory Board of Dad's Club, Inc. a 501(c)(3) non-profit organization. Of note, he has also been the president of the Oak Ridge, NC, Business Network International (BNI) chapter, "Triad Biz-Links."

Tom has been the keynote speaker at many corporate and educational events and has traveled internationally as a business success coach, motivational speaker, and Internet consultant. He has trained in coliseums and arenas, speaking to groups of more than 15,000 people at a time and has provided personalized training to as few as one to three people in a classroom setting.

A focal point of his instruction has been teaching business owners and decision makers how to apply technology to their companies to increase their efficiency, productivity, and profitability.